Contents

To Anthony Morris O.P.
and 'the group' of 1966

Preface

One does not find many books on Dominican spirituality. As a young friar I was taught to be rather suspicious of spirituality. It was seen as an invention of the sixteenth century, when the beautiful unity and synthesis of Medieval Christian thought was lost, splintered into the distinct disciplines of theology, philosophy, ethics, biblical study and spirituality. 'Spirituality' suggested complex techniques for getting in touch with God. It was not our sort of thing at all.

In this book Paul Murray O.P. shows that there is indeed such a thing as 'Dominican spirituality'. It is not about special ways of praying. It is about being alive in God and for others. It is from this life that our preaching springs. This wonderful book begins with a quotation from the second Master of the Order, Blessed Jordan of Saxony, in which he talks of the gospel as the new wine, 'the wine of everlasting joy'. And the book concludes with the fourteenth-century Dominican mystic, St Catherine of Siena, advising her brothers: 'Let us behave like the drunkard who does not think of himself but only of the wine he has drunk and of the wine that remains to be drunk!'

Surprisingly and refreshingly, the drinking of wine emerges as a key metaphor for our earliest brothers and sisters. They clearly enjoyed a good drink. Indeed St Dominic once, after a late night conference, insisted to his sisters that they 'drink deeply', and they all did! Jordan of Saxony, when he preached in England, compared God's longing for our company with a friend who wants to share a drink: 'Nowadays people say, "I think it would be great if you could come to me and have a drink with me." And it's just like that with the Lord.' Drinking wine suggests the exuberant and ecstatic quality of our relationship with God. We are carried outside ourselves, and become self-forgetful, joyful.

Drinking frees us from inhibition, and these early friars and sisters were amazingly free. They preached the gospel of Christ's freedom. 'For freedom Christ has set us free.' (Galatians 5.1). And so they could only be convincing witnesses if they were seen to be free men and women. Dominic himself was described as 'stupefyingly free.' He made an amazing innovation to religious life in insisting that the Constitutions did not bind the brethren under pain of sin, because we 'are not slaves under the law, but free under grace'. He threatened that if any of the brethren began to think that failures in religious observance were sins, then he would personally go around every community and scratch out all the rules. At the heart of this freedom was a confidence in God which led to a confidence in the brethren. How could they be entrusted with preaching the gospel if they were not trusted to use their freedom maturely? It is this confidence that is at the heart of Dominican democracy. Dominic believed that every brother must have his voice in the shaping of our common life.

Murray shows that at the heart of this Dominican spirituality was a profound joy, not just in God but in each other and in the people whom they met. One cannot be a preacher of the good news and be miserable. So the fraternity of the Order should be joyful. Indeed Jordan of Saxony, one of the most lovable and loved of the early friars, even took the gospel phrase 'Enter into the joy of your Lord' (Matthew 25.21) to be an invitation to become a Dominican, an interpretation which would not be universally shared! In the Dialogues God tells Catherine of Siena that Dominic built the ship that is his Order as 'very spacious' and 'very happy' so that 'both the perfect and the not-so-perfect fare well on this ship'.

The foundations of this joy were fraternity, prayer and study. Prayer, in the Dominican tradition, has usually been seen as essentially simple. We talk to God as to a friend; we spontaneously share with God what ever is on our minds, our joys and fears, asking for what we desire and giving thanks for what we receive.

Study also is seen not as a severe and cold intellectual discipline. St Thomas Aquinas, the scholar *par excellence*, is frequently described by Bernard Gui, his biographer, as 'the happy teacher'. Thomas believed that anyone who lacked a sense of joy and could not enjoy jokes was morally unsound. Play is necessary for human life. Study transforms the whole of one's humanity. It opens one's mind and heart to other people. It frees one from slavishly following the crowd, so that one dares to think for oneself. It prepares one to find joy in God's presence. Indeed the whole of ethics, according to Aquinas, is a journey on the path to happiness. Study is seen also as part of our journey to God, sanctifying our minds and hearts.

Murray shows us the profound humanity of these early friars and sisters. They were down to earth and vital. This is a spirituality which is rooted in our lives, in our fundamental desires, in our pain and joy, in our humanity. Dominic's opposition to the heresy of Albigensianism was not that of a narrow fanatic but of a man who whose love of the Creator overflowed in a love of everything to which God gave existence. He could not accept their rejection of the goodness of creation. He opposed them not with the threat of the Inquisition, which did not even exist in his time, but with argument and with persuasion.

THE NEW WINE OF DOMINICAN SPIRITUALITY

I am delighted that Paul Murray shares with us in this book his understanding of Dominican spirituality. It is urgently needed today in a Church which sometimes tends to be gloomy and pessimistic, introverted and fearful. None of us can be credible witnesses to the gospel unless we are infected with something of the joy and freedom which we encounter in this book. If we drink the new wine of the gospel, then it should loosen our tongues to speak of God.

When I lived in Rome and had to prepare a lecture or write a letter to the Order, then I always invited Paul to come and share a pizza and a bottle of wine, not then realizing that this was an expression of Dominican spirituality! I told him what I was thinking of writing about and he would come to the restaurant armed with notes, quotations and poems, which he would declaim as I took copious notes. I owe a deep debt of gratitude to him for all the inspiration that he gave to me and that he now shares with others.

Timothy Radcliffe O.P.

Acknowledgements

Since the Dominican identity is so intimately bound up with the mission of the Order it is no accident that some of the most helpful commentators on the spirituality of the Order have been historians. Among those of my own generation, three names in particular stand out, all three Dominicans: Vladimir Koudelka, Simon Tugwell, and Guy Bedouelle. Although what I have attempted in this work is to put forward my own understanding of the Dominican spiritual tradition, I find it hard to exaggerate the extent of my debt to these scholars, and in particular my debt to the work of Simon Tugwell. A phrase from a medieval author comes to mind. The author, Bernard of Chartres, quite clearly aware of his own limits, but even more aware of the excellence of the work of his predecessors, attributed to them his happy capacity to perceive certain things. 'We are,' he remarked, and the phrase is memorable, 'dwarves mounted on the shoulders of giants.'

With Continuum I have been fortunate twice over, first by having the book accepted by my publisher of choice, and then by receiving all the practical help and encouragement I needed. I am especially grateful to Patricia Hardcastle for her scrupulous and thoughtful copy-editing and to Ben Hayes for his kindness and patience. The first chapter of the present work draws on the text of an address I gave to the General Chapter of the Dominican Order held at Providence College, Rhode Island, July 2001. Originally entitled 'Recovering the Contemplative Dimension' the text was subsequently published as a small booklet in 2003 and given the title *Preachers at Prayer*. I am grateful to Dominican Publications, Dublin, for permission to quote from this booklet. Other sections of the present work appeared originally as articles but in different forms. See 'Dominicans and Happiness', *Dominican Ashram*, 19, 3 (September 2000) pp. 120–42; 'Dominicans Drinking: A Neglected Image of the Holy Preaching', *Religious Life Review*, 41, 216 (Sept/Oct 2002) pp. 272–83; ' "Eat the Book": Study in the Dominican Tradition', *Angelicum*, 81 fasc.2 (2004) pp. 405–30. Grateful acknowledgement is also made to Faber and Faber Ltd. for permission to quote from T. S. Eliot's poem 'To Walter de la Mare' in *The Complete Poems and Plays of T. S. Eliot* (London 1969) and from W. H. Auden's poem 'September 2, 1939' in *Another Time* (London 1940).

I am happy to express here my thanks to those friends and colleagues who graciously read parts of the manuscript or responded to particular queries I sent their way: Jeremy Driscoll, O.S.B., Bob Ombres, O.P., Margaret Atkins, Dr Don Briel, Kate and Louis Marcelin-Rice, Mark O'Brien, O.P., Paul-Bernard Hodel, O.P., and Susan Portieri. In conclusion, I wish also to express, however inadequately, my gratitude to my longtime confrère and friend, Luke Dempsey, O.P. for his unfailing support.

Introduction

The Christian Gospel invites us to taste a new wine – a 'wine', in Jordan of Saxony's phrase, 'of everlasting joy'.[1] It is a wine which initiates us into a life which is, on the one hand, something very simple and fraternal, and yet, on the other hand, something so new and so extraordinary there are hardly words to express it. Today, as in every age, a constant temptation for preachers or ministers of the Gospel, and indeed for believers of all kinds, is to water down this 'wine' of the Gospel with bland ways of thinking and speaking, and to join those among our contemporaries who are leaning, as it were, on the sad 'bar-counter' of average addiction, or average distraction, a place or state of soul tellingly described for us here by the poet, W.H. Auden:

> Faces along the bar
> Cling to their average day:
> The lights must never go out,

---

[1] Jordan of Saxony, *Epistola XXXV*, in *Beati Iordani De Saxonia Epistulae*, Angelus Walz O.P. (ed.), MOPH XXIII (Rome 1951) p. 42.

THE NEW WINE OF DOMINICAN SPIRITUALITY

> The music must always play ...
> Lest we should see where we are,
> Lost in a haunted wood,
> Children afraid of the night
> Who have never been happy or good.[2]

One reason, perhaps, why so many in society today feel unfulfilled and are not 'happy' is because the vision of life which we are offered, or which - sad to say - we allow to be imposed on us, is one that is restricted to a pragmatic, one-dimensional view of the world. We live in thrall to what the Australian novelist Patrick White has called 'the exaltation of the average'.[3] White himself, quickened into a state of near panic by this situation, writes: 'I wanted to discover the extraordinary behind the ordinary, the mystery and poetry which alone could make bearable the lives of [ordinary] people, and my own life.'[4] Over the centuries, through generation after generation, right up into our own age, the mystery and poetry of the Christian gospel has inspired many different paths of spirituality. The Dominican path - the Dominican way - is only one path among many. But it is a path which is truly 'broad and joyous',[5]

---

[2] W.H. Auden, 'September 1', 1939, in *Another Time* (London 1940) p. 113.

[3] P. White, 'The Prodigal Son', in *Australian Letters*, vol. I, 3, (1958) p. 39.

[4] *ibid.*, p. 17.

[5] These two beautiful adjectives 'broad' and 'joyous' ('*larga*' and '*gioconda*') emerge in the dialogue between St Catherine of Siena and God the Father when the Father speaks directly to Catherine about the nature of the Dominican Order. See *Il Dialogo della divina providenza*, CLVIII, G. Cavallini (ed.) (Rome 1968) p. 462.

and it has been for myself no small joy to have attempted, in this present work, to make audible some of the different voices from the first two centuries of the Dominican tradition.

Naturally, in one limited work, it will not be possible to present anything like a detailed or comprehensive picture of the depth and range of Dominican spirituality. My more modest aim is to offer an understanding, first of all, of the nature of Dominican spirituality in general, and then to try to name and celebrate one or two aspects of the Dominican way which have not so far received the attention they deserve: the unmistakable joy and exuberance of the early Dominicans, for example, and the importance given, in their lives as preachers, to becoming drunk on the Word – themes which, I am persuaded, reveal something fundamental about the Dominican character and style. The motto of the Dominican Order is 'Truth', and that suggests a particular commitment to, and respect for, the life of the mind. But why should Dominicans regard the awakening of the mind as of such importance? And why should study, or hard-headed thinking, be considered in some way crucial for spiritual growth and for the life of the preacher? These questions are taken up and reflected on in the chapter entitled ' "Eat the Book": Study in the Dominican Tradition.' They are questions which, I believe, are important not only for Dominicans but for almost anyone today who is interested in spirituality and has been inspired by the truth of the Gospel.

The tradition under review has its roots far back in the Middle Ages. But it is remarkable, at times, how a particular letter, or treatise, or homily, which was first read or heard in the thirteenth or fourteenth century, can today sound so contemporary. One reason for this is the fact that the tradition itself is not simply a series of texts buried under the dust of time, and waiting to be dug up and dissected by devoted scholars and archaeologists. No – it is a *living* tradition, a tradition which has, in spite of innumerable difficulties and setbacks, survived into our own age. So, in turning our attention back now to the Dominican past, our intention is not in any way to escape from the demands of the present, and become mere archaeologists of a tradition, but rather, in the brilliant phrase of the poet, Rainer Maria Rilke, to become 'seekers of *the inner future* ... [of the] past'.[6]

---

[6] Rainer Maria Rilke, *Letter to Lou Andreas-Salomé, August 15, 1903*, in *Letters of Rainer Maria Rilke* (New York 1945) p. 127. Italics added.

1

What is Dominican Spirituality?

'The well-known is what we have yet to learn.'[1]

T.S. Eliot

Sometimes the traits distinctive of a particular group of people are the very traits which remain invisible to the group itself. Jorge Luis Borges has observed in one of his essays that in the Koran there is, surprisingly, not a single camel mentioned.[2] Outsiders, concerned in their work to depict the Islamic world, or the Arab world, might well be inclined to fill pages with references to camels - 'caravans of camels, on every page.'[3] In contrast, the people actually living and working with camels, day in day out, don't necessarily feel the need to talk about them. They are

[1] T.S. Eliot, *To Walter de la Mare*, in *The Complete Poems and Plays of T.S. Eliot* (London 1969) p. 204.

[2] Jorge Luis Borges, *The Argentine Writer and Tradition*, in *Labyrinths*, D.A. Yates (ed.) (New York 1962) pp. 171-9.

[3] *ibid.*, p. 175.

unaware that the camel in their life is, to the outsider, or to those who have come to know them well, a distinguishing mark.

When, in the thirteenth century, the Dominican Order was founded, it would never have occurred to the first Friars Preachers to spell out, in a detailed and precise manner, the distinctive character of their spirituality.[4] For a start, the word 'spirituality', as we understand it today, was not part of the medieval vocabulary. And, in any case, the primary concern of the early Dominicans was not to announce the arrival of a new spirituality, but rather, simply, in a difficult and testing hour, to preach the good news of the Gospel. That said, it is by no means impossible, at this late stage in the Order's history, to indicate a number of underlying themes and concerns, ideas and reactions, which recur in the writings of Dominicans. And since, in relation to preaching and prayer, for example, they recur with a notable frequency, there is some reason to regard them as typically Dominican.

[4] I refer here only to the friars, the Dominican men. But it should be noted that Dominic was instrumental also in the foundation of a number of monasteries for enclosed contemplative women. Already in the Middle Ages, various lay groups and confraternities came to be regarded as part of the Dominican family; and, in more recent centuries, a number of active, non-cloistered congregations of Dominican women have also emerged. See Vladimir Koudelka O.P., *Dominic and Women*, in *Dominic* (London 1997) pp. 159-71; Guy Bedouelle O.P., *The Nuns* and *A Place for the Laity* in *Saint Dominic: The Grace of the Word* (San Francisco 1987) pp. 204-15; Simon Tugwell O.P., *Dominican Nuns and Laity*, in *Early Dominicans: Selected Writings* (New York 1982) pp. 27-31.

Gospel Prayer, Gospel Spirit

One of the great merits, in my view, of the Dominican contemplative tradition is its dogged resistance to the esoteric aura or spiritual glamour that tends to surround the subject of contemplation. The well-known preacher in the English Province, the Northern Irishman Vincent McNabb, for example, with characteristic good humour, liked now and again to bring the subject of contemplation back down from the high clouds of mysticism to the plain earth of Gospel truth. Concerning the question of prayer, for example, as presented in the parable of the Pharisee and the Publican, McNabb writes:

> The Publican did not know he was justified. If you had asked him, 'Can you pray?' he would have said, 'No, I cannot pray. I was thinking of asking the Pharisee. He seems to know all about it. I could only say I was a sinner. My past is so dreadful. I cannot imagine myself praying. I am better at stealing.'[5]

In *The Nine Ways of Prayer* we are afforded a glimpse of St Dominic himself repeating the Publican's prayer while lying down prostrate on the ground before God. 'His heart,' we are told, 'would be pricked with compunction, and he would blush at himself and say, sometimes loudly enough for it actually to be heard, the words from the Gospel, "Lord, be merciful to me, a sinner." '[6] Without exception I find that, in the prayer-lives of the Dominican preachers I most admire, there is always something of

[5] Vincent McNabb O.P., *The Craft of Prayer* (London 1935) p. 77.
[6] Prayer 2, *The Nine Ways of Prayer* [of St Dominic], in S. Tugwell, *Early Dominicans,* p. 95.

that common neediness, and that Gospel simplicity. When at prayer these preachers are not afraid to speak to God directly, as to a friend. But always they return instinctively to the straightforward Gospel prayer of petition. Here is Aquinas, for example:

> I come before you as a sinner, O God, Source of all mercy. I am unclean, I beseech you to cleanse me. O Sun of Justice, give sight to a blind man ... O King of Kings, clothe one who is destitute.

> Almighty, everlasting God, you see that I am coming to the sacrament of your only Son, our Lord Jesus Christ. I come to it as a sick man to the life-giving healer, as one unclean to the source of mercy ... as one who is poor and destitute to the Lord of heaven and earth.[7]

'Sometimes,' a thirteenth-century Dominican homily makes bold to declare, 'a man is in a state of damnation before he begins his prayer, and before he is finished he is in a state of salvation!'[8] The preacher of this homily, William Peraldus, in answer to the question 'why ought everyone to be glad to learn how to pray?' says something which we almost never hear stated three centuries later. For, by that time, prayer, in its most authentic form, was generally thought to be something very difficult to achieve. But Peraldus, the Dominican, states without the least hesitation or self-consciousness, 'Prayer is such an

---

[7] Prayers I and II, in *Piae preces*; 'Appendix' in *Opuscula alia dubia*, III, *Opera omnia*, vol. XXIV (Parma 1869) pp. 241–2.

[8] William Peraldus, *Sermon on Prayer*, in S. Tugwell, *Early Dominicans*, p. 168.

easy job!'[9] That statement was repeated almost verbatim in a Dominican homily preached several centuries later in England by Vincent McNabb. 'Prayer,' McNabb declared, 'is almost the easiest thing in the world.'[10] And again: 'If our Blessed Lord tells the Apostles they should pray *always* ... [p]rayer must be something extraordinarily easy – at least some form of prayer.'[11] McNabb's assertion here may sound at first naive. But it draws its authority, I believe, from the Gospel itself. For is it not the case that we are encouraged in the Gospel by Christ to pray with great simplicity of heart and straightforwardness? When, over the years, Dominicans have found themselves confronted with detailed methods and techniques of meditation, and with long lists of instructions of what to do in meditation and what not to do, their reaction has almost always been the same: they instinctively feel that something has gone wrong.[12]

[9] *ibid.*, p. 167.

[10] *Prayer – How Easy It Is*, in *The Craft of Prayer* p. 64.

[11] *ibid.* That qualification, 'at least some form of prayer,' draws attention to the fact that there are, of course, particular stages or occasions in the lives of all Christians when prayer is anything but easy. It is no surprise, therefore, that in a Dominican text such as *The Dialogue* of St Catherine of Siena, for example, we find reference made to 'all sorts of struggles and annoyances' in the life of prayer. See *The Dialogue* 65, trans., S. Noffke O.P. (New York 1980) p. 122. That said, however, prayer in *The Dialogue* itself has a marked simplicity, and assumes again and again the two most basic forms of Gospel prayer: petition and thanksgiving.

[12] This point is made forcefully by Simon Tugwell in an illuminating article entitled 'A Dominican Theology of Prayer', *Dominican Ashram*, I, 3 (1982) 128-44.

The reaction of Bede Jarrett, the English Dominican, is typical. In one place he notes, with real regret, how on occasion prayer can become 'reduced to hard and fast rules', and can be so 'mapped-out' and 'regimented' that, 'it hardly seems at all to be the language of the heart'. When this happens, in the memorable words of Jarrett, 'All adventure has gone, all the personal touches, and all the contemplation. We are too worried and harassed to think of God. The instructions are so detailed and insistent that we forget what we are trying to learn. As a consequence, we get bored and so no doubt does God.'[13]

St Dominic's 'Special Grace'

No devotional text or spiritual treatise was ever composed by Dominic for his brethren in the Order. The one testament he left behind - and it is a magnificent document - is the Book of Constitutions. Dominic was a preacher first and last - not a writer. And yet, even at this distance in time, there are available to us within the tradition a surprising number of details concerning his way of prayer and contemplation. One reason for this is Dominic's own extraordinary temperament. He possessed an exuberance of nature that, far from being suppressed by a life of prayer and penance, seems in fact to have been wonderfully awakened and released. He was a man, as Cardinal Villot once remarked, 'stupefyingly

---

[13] See *Contemplation*, in *Meditations for Layfolk* (London 1946) p. 182, cited in S. Tugwell, 'A Dominican Theology of Prayer', p. 129.

free'.[14] At prayer in particular he could hardly, it seems, contain himself. Often he would cry out to God at the top of his voice. As a result, even his private prayer was a kind of open book to his brethren. At night, when he was alone in the church, his voice would often be heard echoing throughout the entire convent.

So Dominic prays with all that he is - body and soul. He prays privately with intense and humble devotion. And, with that same deep faith and profound emotion, he prays in public the prayer of the Mass. Although the intensity of Dominic's faith and feeling may be unusual, as well as the extraordinary length of his night vigils, for the rest his prayer seems indistinguishable from that of any ordinary devout Christian man or woman. His prayer is never in any way esoteric. It is always simple, always ecclesial.

Obviously, at the core of St Dominic's life, there was a profound contemplative love of God. But reading through the early accounts of his prayer-life, what also immediately impresses is the place accorded to *others* - to the afflicted and oppressed - within the act of contemplation itself. One phrase associated with Dominicans since the thirteenth century (and which, by now, has almost become a Dominican motto) is the Latin phrase '*contemplata aliis tradere*': 'to pass on to others what we ourselves have contemplated.' But the '*alii*' - the others - are not simply the passive recipients of Dominic's graced preaching. Even before the actual moment of preaching

[14] '*Homelia in Basilica Sanctae Sabinae*,' ASOP, 39 (July-September 1970) p. 543.

(when Dominic becomes a kind of channel of grace) these people – the afflicted and oppressed – inhabit the inmost core of his spirit. They form part even of the '*contemplata*' in '*contemplata aliis tradere*'. Jordan of Saxony writes:

> God had given [Dominic] a special grace to weep for sinners and for the afflicted and oppressed; he bore their distress in the inmost shrine of his compassion, and the warm sympathy he felt for them in his heart spilled over in the tears which flowed from his eyes.[15]

In part, of course, this means simply that, when he prays, Dominic remembers to intercede for those people he knows to be in need, and for sinners especially. But there is something more, some 'special grace', to use Jordan's phrase. The wound of knowledge that opens up Dominic's mind and heart in contemplation, allowing him with an awesome unprotectedness to experience his neighbour's pain and his neighbour's need, cannot be accounted for simply by certain crowding memories of pain observed or by his own natural sympathy. The apostolic wound Dominic receives, which enables him to act and to preach, is a contemplative wound.

Writing at St Jacques in Paris, sometime in the early thirteenth century, an anonymous Dominican author noted that 'among the things a man ought to see [in

---

[15] Jordan of Saxony, *Libellus de principiis ordinis praedicatorum*, 12, in MOPH, XVI, M-H. Laurent O.P. (ed.) (Rome 1935) p. 32; trans., S. Tugwell in *Jordan of Saxony: On the Beginnings of the Order of Preachers* (Dublin 1982) p. 3.

contemplation] are the needs of his neighbour' and also 'how great is the weakness of every human being'.[16] And he noted further: 'Understand from what you know about yourself the condition of your neighbour (*Intellige ex te ipso quae sunt proximi tui*). And what you see in Christ and in the world and in your neighbour, write that in your heart.'[17] These lines are memorable for the compassionate attention they give to the neighbour in the context of contemplation. But I would like to think also that their emphasis on true self-knowledge, and their simple openness to Christ, to the neighbour, and to the world, strike a distinctly Dominican note. The passage ends with a simple but impressive reference to the task of preaching. We are exhorted by our author first of all to understand ourselves and be attentive to all that we see in the world around us and in our neighbour, and to reflect deep within our hearts on the things that we have observed. But then we are told to go out and preach: 'First see, then write, then send ... What is needed first is study, then reflection within the heart, and then preaching.'[18]

Preaching as a Spiritual Task

Not every form of contemplation was enthusiastically embraced by the first Dominicans. In fact, in the *Vitae*

[16] '*Vidit Jacob ...*': '*Expositio I super Apocalypsim,*' ch. I, edited under the name of Thomas Aquinas, in *Opuscula alia dubia*, II, *Opera omnia*, vol XXIII (Parma 1869) p. 335.

[17] *ibid.*, p. 334.

[18] *ibid.*, p. 335.

Fratrum, there has survived a vivid account of one unfortunate friar who, we're told, very nearly lost his faith from too much 'contemplation'![19] In similar vein, Humbert of Romans, in a study of enormous length entitled, *Treatise on the Formation of Preachers*, openly complains about those people whose 'sole passion is for contemplation'. These men seek out, he says, a 'hidden life of quiet' or 'a retired place for contemplation' and then 'refuse to respond to the summons to be useful to others by preaching'.[20]

The word 'contemplation' in these early Dominican texts does not possess the rather esoteric and high mystical character which it would later acquire in the sixteenth century. The word, it is true, can sometimes be linked with the notions of recollection and retirement, but it tends to have a much more plain and down-to-earth connotation. Often it can mean, in fact, little more than a simple act of prayerful attention or prayerful study. (In modern times, to add to the confusion, we tend to use the word 'contemplation' as a basic synonym for prayer itself.)

Now, obviously, Humbert of Romans is not intending to set up, as contraries to one another, the life of prayer and the life of preaching. 'Since human effort can achieve nothing without the help of God,' he writes, 'the most important thing of all for a preacher is that he should

[19] Gerald de Frachet, *Vitae Fratrum*, III, 15, MOPH, I, B.M. Reichert O.P. (ed.) (Louvain 1896) p. 112.
[20] Humbert of Romans, *Treatise on the Formation of Preachers*, IV, xvii, 193. (Humbert is quoting from St Gregory the Great's *Pastoral Rule*.) See S. Tugwell, *Early Dominicans*, p. 242.

have recourse to prayer.'[21] But the life of prayer and contemplation, which the early Dominicans recommend, is one which would compel us, in Humbert's phrase, to 'come out into the open',[22] compel us, that is, to set about the task of preaching.

That there should be an Order in the Church devoted exclusively to itinerant preaching might seem obvious to us today. But, in the early thirteenth century, the travelling around of the first Friars Preachers was considered 'frivolous' by many. The friars tended, in fact, to be perceived as a group of irresponsible 'gyrovagues' and their active preaching ministry dismissed as if it were beneath the dignity of serious religious. In their defence, however, a Dominican author, Thomas of Cantimpré, felt constrained to challenge this negative assessment. In a work entitled, *Defense of the Mendicants*, he wrote:

> Well, my brethren, you need not be ashamed to be called or to be gyrovagues. You are in the company of St Paul, the teacher of the nations ... While they [the monks] sit in their monasteries ... you go touring round with Paul, doing the job you have been given to do. And I am hopeful that if you suffer oppression in the world, you will still have peace in Christ, perhaps as much peace or more than they have who sit grumbling in their place of quiet.[23]

Another Dominican of the thirteenth century, Stephen of Bourbon, tells us of a certain novice of the Order who

[21] *ibid.*, I, vii; S. Tugwell, *Early Dominicans*, 96, p. 209.

[22] *ibid.*, IV, xvii, 193; S. Tugwell, *Early Dominicans*, p. 242.

[23] Thomas of Cantimpré, *Defense of the Mendicants*, in S. Tugwell, *Early Dominicans*, p. 134.

found himself surrounded, on one occasion, by a group of monks. They criticized the Dominican Order at great length, and tried to persuade him to join their own monastic Order, speaking of it, of course, 'in glowing terms'.[24] But the novice held fast to his vocation. 'He ... asked them whether the Lord Jesus Christ had given us a pattern of right living which excelled all others, and whether his own conduct was to be our rule. They said, "Yes." "So," he replied, "when I read that the Lord Jesus Christ was not a white monk or a black monk, but a poor preacher, I want to follow in his footsteps more than in those of anyone else." '[25]

Probably the most sustained defence of St Dominic's band of preachers – 'this strange new religious Order'[26] – is the treatise on preaching which was composed by Blessed Humbert of Romans. Because the preacher's life was so little understood at that time, and was so often under attack, Humbert, in his treatise, has no hesitation whatever in making the strongest possible case for the preacher's vocation. He is not shy, for example, to assert that, 'preaching should be preferred to all other spiritual exercises by spiritual men who are capable of it'.[27] At

---

[24] See *Miscellaneous Stories*, in S. Tugwell, *Early Dominicans*, p. 139.
[25] *ibid.*
[26] Jordan of Saxony uses this phrase to express the puzzlement some people felt at their first encounter with the Order. See *Jordan of Saxony: On the Beginnings of the Friars Preachers*, p. 19.
[27] Humbert of Romans, *Treatise*, III, xxi, 275; S. Tugwell, *Early Dominicans*, p. 259. On the subject of preaching Yves Congar, enlisting the authority of Humbert of Romans among others, goes so far as to

times, so vivid and so unexpected and colourful are Humbert's arguments in defence of the preacher's task, they impress the modern reader not only as polemical in intention but also as somewhat humorous. Thus, in order to emphasize the importance of preaching in Christ's life and, at the same time, to answer those critics who were inclined to identify religion exclusively with 'being present at divine worship ... haunting churches when the Divine Office is being celebrated',[28] Humbert makes bold to declare:

> When Christ was in this world, he celebrated Mass only once, on Maundy Thursday; we do not read of him ever hearing confessions, he administered few sacraments and those infrequently, he did not very often assist at any canonical divine worship; you will find the same thing is true of all the practices mentioned above, except prayer and preaching. And once he started preaching, we find in the gospels that he is presented as having devoted his whole life to preaching, even more than to prayer.[29]

It was not only the monks who had difficulty coming to terms with 'this new and un-heard of kind of religious

<hr />

cont.

claim that 'if in one country Mass was celebrated for thirty years without preaching and in another there was preaching for thirty years without the Mass, people would be more Christian in the country where there was preaching'. See Yves Congar, *Sacramental Worship and Preaching*, in *The Renewal of Preaching: Theory and Practice*, K. Rahner (ed.) (New York 1993), p. 62.

[28] *ibid.*, III, xxi, 268; S. Tugwell, *Early Dominicans*, p. 258.

[29] *ibid.*, III, xxi, 269; S. Tugwell, *Early Dominicans*, pp. 258-9.

Order'.[30] A pious woman of Lombardy, when she first encountered some of the preaching brethren, was utterly scandalized. According to Gerard de Frachet, 'when she noticed how young and good-looking they were, and how fine their habit was, she despised them, reckoning that people like that touring round the world could not last long in chastity.'[31] Needless to say, the early Dominicans were not unaware of the risks they were taking. By the very nature of their apostolate, they were a lot more likely to meet with temptation than were those religious who remained enclosed within the walls of monasteries. Humbert of Romans speaks explicitly, in his treatise on preaching, of 'the risk of sin' in the preacher's life, and of the danger of 'rushing into dangerous occasions of sin in one's eagerness to win the souls of others'.[32] Nevertheless, in spite of this danger, Blessed Humbert clearly believes that there are times in the preacher's life when great risks must be taken. And so, with regard to those men who are called to preach the Word, but who 'hold back because they are afraid of the kind of sins which will unavoidably occur in the course of the preacher's active life',[33] he writes: 'Is it not better that men should work, even if they are going to pick up a certain amount of dust

[30] The phrase is quoted in *The Life of Dominic* by Jean de Mailly. See S. Tugwell, *Early Dominicans*, p. 58.

[31] *Vitae Fratrum*, I, 6, xiv (following Reichert's MS C); trans., in S. Tugwell, *Early Dominicans*, p. 137.

[32] Humbert of Romans, *Treatise*, IV, xix, 237; S. Tugwell, *Early Dominicans*, p. 252.

[33] *ibid.*, IV, xvii, 194; S. Tugwell, *Early Dominicans*, p. 242.

18

as they work, than that they should always stay quite clean and at home?'[34] Having made this statement, however, Humbert adds, in a later paragraph, and with a down-to-earth honesty and common sense equal to his daring: 'A wise preacher ought to return to himself after going out to preach, and carefully examine everything that has happened to him, so that he can wash away any defilement that he has incurred and repair anything that has got broken. He should be like a traveller who cleans and mends his shoes when he arrives at a hospice, so that he can journey better thereafter.'[35]

The World within God's Hand

In some religious traditions, the contemplative life implied an almost complete turning away from the world, and in the case of certain ascetic religious, of a

---

[34] *ibid.*, IV, xvii, 194; S. Tugwell, *Early Dominicans*, p. 243. A similar comment was made by the popular Dominican preacher, Blessed Jordan of Rivalto. It is true, he admits, that the young Friars Preachers will not be spotless all the time, given the nature of their work. But he asks that people not judge them too harshly: 'being here among the people, seeing the things of the world, it is impossible for them not to get a bit dirty. They are men of flesh and blood like you, and in the freshness of youth – it is a wonder that they are as clean as they are. This is no place for monks! We are certainly here among you for our own good, but it is much more for your sake that we are here ...' *Prediche*, D.M. Manni (ed.) (Florence 1739) p. 9, cited in S. Tugwell O.P., *The Way of the Preacher* (London 1981) pp. 50-1.

[35] Humbert of Romans, *Treatise*, IV, xix, 238; S. Tugwell, *Early Dominicans*, pp. 252-3.

rejection not only of their immediate family and friends, but also of people in general, or at least those who appeared to be dominated by weakness or by worldly passion. Fortunately, however, the impulse towards contemplation in the lives of our best-known Dominican preachers and saints was never characterized by that sort of rigid, judgmental attitude. The contemplative apostle in the Dominican tradition, the authentic preacher, does not call down curses on the sinful world. But, instead, conscious of his or her own weakness, and humbly identified, therefore, with the world's need, the Dominican calls down a blessing.

In an unusually striking moment in *The Dialogue* of St Catherine of Siena, the saint is asked by God the Father to lift up her eyes to him so that he might demonstrate, in some way, the extent of his passionate care for the whole world. 'Look at my hand,' the Father says to her. When Catherine does this, she sees at once – and the vision must have astonished her – the entire world being somehow held up and enclosed in God's hand. Then, the Father says to her: 'My daughter, see now and know that no-one can be taken away from me … They are mine. I created them and I love them ineffably. And so, in spite of their wickedness, I will be merciful to them … and I will grant what you have asked me with such love and sorrow.'[36]

In contemplation we seek to turn our whole attention to God. God is, therefore, the supreme object of our

---

[36] *The Dialogue,* 18, pp. 56-7.

regard. But there is another way, I would suggest, of approaching the mystery of God and of thinking about religious experience. God's Word, though utterly transcendent in its source, has come down into the world, and has taken flesh. Instead, therefore, of thinking always of the individual contemplative looking *at* God, and in some sense looking away from things, and away from the world, we can think of the ecstasy of prayer in reverse: the contemplative coming out *from* God *towards* things, and of being called to share in God's gaze – with God, that is, in some sense as 'Subject' – God looking at the world and at things *with* us and *through* us. 'The real aim,' Simone Weil remarks, 'is not to see God in all things; it is that God through us should see the things that we see. God has to be on the side of the *subject*.'[37] In the life of grace, therefore, in the Incarnation, the first initiative always belongs to God. And that is why, both in our work and in our prayer, we soon come to realize that Christ is much more than the object of our regard. He is the Word alive within us, the *friend* 'in whom we live and move and have our being'. And thus, we can make bold to say, echoing the First Letter of St John: This is contemplation – this is contemplative love – not so much that we contemplate God, but that God has first contemplated us, and that

[37] Simone Weil, *The Notebooks*, vol. 2 (New York 1956) p. 358. Italics added. Weil also writes: 'we imitate the descending movement of God ... [when we] turn ourselves toward the world' (p. 358). There is a telling reference to God as 'the essential subject' in S. Tugwell, *The Way of the Preacher*, p. 27.

now *in* us, in some sense, and even *through* us, as part of the mystery of his risen life in the church, he contemplates the world.

In one of his books, the French Dominican theologian, Yves Congar, deliberately takes to task those people – some of them monks and priests – whose passion for the Absolute tends to make them indifferent to the world and to 'the true inwardness of things', to the fact that 'things exist in themselves, with their own proper nature and needs'.[38] Reflecting on this matter, Congar highlights what he considers to be an important, if unexpected, *lay quality* in the Dominican vision of Aquinas. In Congar's opinion, someone who is 'authentically lay',[39] such as Aquinas, is 'one for whom, through the very work which God has entrusted to him, the substance of things in themselves is real and interesting'.[40] Congar strikes a similar note in a letter written to a fellow Dominican in 1959. Expressing a certain disinterest in what he referred to as 'the distinction "contemplative/active life"', Congar writes:

> If my God is the God of the Bible, the living God, the 'I am, I was, I am coming,' then God is inseparable from the world and from human beings … My action, then, consists in handing myself over to my God, who allows me to be the link for his divine activity regarding the world and other people. My relationship to God is not that of a cultic act,

[38] Yves Congar O.P., *Lay People in the Church: A Study for a Theology of Laity* (London 1959) pp. 17–18.
[39] *ibid.*, p. 21
[40] *ibid.*, p. 17.

which rises up from me to Him, but rather that of a faith by which I hand myself over to the action of the living God, communicating himself according to his plan, to the world and to other human beings. I can only place myself faithfully before God, and offer the fullness of my being and my resources so that I can be there where God awaits me, the link between this action of God and the world.[41]

Reading this extract from Congar's letter, I am at once reminded of one of the most remarkable visions of St Catherine of Siena, a vision in which St Dominic appears precisely as a kind of 'link' between God's action and the world. Catherine reported to her Dominican friend, Bartolomeo, that first of all she saw the Son of God coming forth from the mouth of the Eternal Father. And then, to her amazement, she saw, emerging from the Father's breast, 'the most blessed Patriarch Dominic'.[42] In order to 'dispel her amazement' the Father then said to her: 'Just as this Son of mine, by nature ... spoke out before the world ... so too Dominic, my son by adoption.'[43] The union between Dominic and the Father, in this vision, could hardly be more intimate. But the preacher is not seen here in the usual mode of the contemplative, turning away from the world towards God. Rather, with the Son of God, Dominic is seen coming out from the One who, from the very beginning, 'so loved the world'. In Congar's terms,

---

[41] 'Action et contemplation: D'une lettre du père Congar au père Régamey' (1959), *La Vie spirituelle*, 152, 727 (1998) p. 204.

[42] See Raymond of Capua's *The Life of Catherine of Siena*, trans. C. Kearns O.P. (Wilmington 1980) p. 195.

[43] *ibid.*, p. 21.

Dominic's only action has been to surrender himself, with faith and hope, to the great, saving initiative of God. 'There is only one thing that is real,' Congar writes, 'one thing that is true: to hand oneself over to God!'[44]

This second way of understanding faith-experience, of considering God not so much as an 'object' outside ourselves, for whose greater glory we undertake all our different works, but rather as a 'subject' alive within us and around us, a divine Presence, 'in whom we live and move and have our being', is a notion explored in one of his books by the Trappist monk, Thomas Merton.[45] Inspired – Merton tells us – by something he read in the work of Johannes Tauler, the medieval Dominican mystic and preacher, he makes a distinction between two kinds of intention, a *right* intention and a *simple* intention. When we have a *right* intention, Merton says, 'we seek to do God's will' but 'we consider the work and ourselves apart from God and outside Him'. But 'when we have a *simple* intention, we ... do all that we do not only *for* God but, so to speak, *in* Him. We are more aware of Him who works in us than of ourselves or of our work.'[46] Both of these ways of prayer are manifestly Christian, and both are practiced by Dominicans. But it is the second, I would suggest, which more closely approximates to the preacher's way and to the Dominican spiritual path.

Many years ago I remember hearing on the radio an interview with a world-famous opera singer, and he

[44] Congar, *Action et contemplation*, p. 204.
[45] Thomas Merton, *No Man is an Island* (New York 1955) p. 85.
[46] *ibid*, p. 21.

confessed, during the interview, to having suffered, at certain stages during his career, from stage-fright. The advice he was given by a good friend in order to help him overcome his stage-fright came in two stages. The first time he went to his friend, the advice he received was as follows: 'When you are singing in public, although you will naturally be singing for a particular audience, secretly, in your inner heart, *sing for God.*' This advice was precious advice, and for a time it helped him overcome his nerves. But then, after a while, he began to suffer yet again from stage-fright, and he went back to his friend. On this occasion, the advice he received was wholly unexpected but, in the end, even more helpful. 'When you are singing in public,' his friend said, 'stand up straight, relax, take a deep breath, and *let God sing through you!*' Both of these statements, obviously, have their own wisdom. But it is the second which, if I am not mistaken, strikes the authentic 'Dominican' note. In contrast to a spirituality which would rely perhaps too much on the determination of the *will* to effect changes in the world for the greater glory of God, the Dominican emphasis on *grace* – on the happy recognition, that is, of God's own saving initiative and of God's 'mad' love for the world – makes for a much less uptight and a far more joyful and spontaneous kind of spirituality.[47] 'Activity which is too intentional,' in the view of the Dominican A.D. Sertillanges, 'makes our intelligence less sure and less receptive; if we strive too anxiously, we remain shut up in

---

[47] With regard to this point, Simon Tugwell offers an arresting reflection on the implications of the Dominican theology of grace in *Early Dominicans*, p. 26.

ourselves, whereas to understand is to become *other*, and in happy receptivity to let truth pour in upon us.'[48]

In the Dominican tradition, preaching was always regarded as a spiritual activity, even a contemplative one. '[T]he merit of preaching,' according to Humbert of Romans, 'wins the gift of an increase of interior grace.'[49] But that does not negate the need for a regular prayer life. On the contrary, both for Dominic, and for the early Friars Preachers, speaking about God – '*de Deo*', the grace of preaching – presupposed first speaking with God – '*cum Deo*' – the grace of actual prayer or contemplation.[50] In the apostolic life adopted by the friars, the ecstasy of service or attention to the neighbour was unthinkable without the ecstasy of prayer or attention to God, and vice versa. To become a preacher one did not have to be a

[48] A. D. Sertillanges O.P., *The Intellectual Life*, (Cork 1965) p. 132.

[49] See *Treatise*, I, v, 34; S. Tugwell, *Early Dominicans*, p. 195.

[50] In the *Primitive Constitutions* of the Order (Dist.II., c.31) the early Dominicans were exhorted to be 'like men of the Gospel, following in the footsteps of their Saviour, talking either with God or about God.' The phrase 'with God or about God' (*cum Deo vel de Deo*), which tradition ascribed to the monk Stephen of Muret, was clearly a favourite of Dominic. A number of witnesses at the Bologna Canonization Process refer to it. Three of them, William of Monferrato, Stephen of Spain, and Paul of Venice, when citing the phrase, reverse the order of the words, as if to give priority to preaching, saying that Dominic talked either 'about God or with God' (*de Deo vel cum Deo*). *Acta canonizationis s. Dominici*, nos.13, 37, 41, in MOPH XVI (Rome 1935) pp. 135, 155 and 161. But in the deposition of Brother John of Spain (another of the witnesses at Bologna) we read that Dominic 'rarely spoke except with God in prayer or about God (*cum Deo, scilicet orando, vel de Deo*) and he encouraged the brethren to do the same'. *Ibid.*, XXIX, p. 146.

monk of the desert, or a master of mysticism, or even a saint. But one did have to become, in Humbert of Roman's phrase, at least 'a pray-er first'.[51] As a carrier or bearer of the Word of life to the world, the Dominican needed first to live in intimacy with the Word, and needed also to learn, like St Dominic, to drink deep from the well of Gospel truth. 'For,' as it is made clear in *The Dialogue* of St Catherine of Siena, 'one cannot share what one does not have in oneself.'[52]

Earlier I spoke of the 'lay spirit' in Aquinas – how he showed instinctive interest in, and respect for, all the *things* of this world. But it should be remembered also that when, in the *Summa*, Aquinas discusses the contemplative life, he gives enormous weight and importance to what he calls the contemplation of '*eternal* things'. He writes: 'The contemplative life consists in a certain liberty of spirit. Thus Gregory says that *the contemplative life produces a certain freedom of mind, because it considers eternal things, not temporal.*'[53] That 'freedom of mind' is not something reserved for enclosed contemplatives. Preachers, in fact, are in need of that freedom more, perhaps, than anyone. For, without it, they risk becoming prisoners of the spirit of the age, and of the

---

[51] Humbert is citing Augustine. He writes that the man who gets people to listen to him 'should have no doubt that it is thanks to his devout prayers rather than to his well-trained fluency in speech ... So let him be a pray-er first, and then a teacher.' See *Treatise*, IV, xix, 233; S. Tugwell, *Early Dominicans*, p. 252.

[52] *The Dialogue*, 85, p. 157.

[53] ST, II II, q.182, a.1, ad.2. Italics added.

27

fashions of the age. And what they preach, in the end, will not be the Word of God, but instead some word or some ideology of their own. And *that* word, *that* message, will be of little use to the world, even if it is carried to the furthest frontiers of human need. For to really 'come out into the open', what is required first, as the Gospel reminds us, is to make a journey *within*. 'God,' Eckhart says: 'is in, we are out. God is at home, we are abroad ... "God leads the just through narrow paths to the highway that they may come out into the open."' [54]

The Question of Identity

I remember, just after I had joined the Dominican Order, when I was still a novice, putting a question about the distinctive character of Dominican spirituality to one of the older priests in the community, a wonderful man called Cathal Hutchinson. My question was a typical novice question, as earnest and sincere as it was naive. 'What,' I asked, 'is the secret of Dominican contemplation?' Father Cathal hesitated a moment. He smiled at me. Then he said: 'Brother Paul, never tell the Carmelites or the Jesuits, but we have no secret other than the Gospel secret!' The reply was, I think, both wise and good-humoured. But it was also deliberately evasive, and

---

[54] Sermon Sixty-Nine, in *Meister Eckhart: Sermons and Treatises*, vol. II [German Sermons and Treatises], M.O'C. Walshe (ed.) (Longmeade 1981) p. 169. It is worth noting that Eckhart's splendid phrase 'come out into the open' was also used by Humbert of Romans in his *Treatise*, IV, xvii, 193; S. Tugwell, *Early Dominicans*, p. 242.

evasive for a reason. Part of the puzzle and fascination of Dominican spirituality is that it cannot easily be held within the categories of spirituality which have been developed since the sixteenth century. That does not mean, of course, that there is no such thing as Dominican spirituality, but only that we must be careful not to impose upon the Dominican past a framework of thought and vision entirely foreign to it.

In the 40 or so years since I was a novice, alongside the ever-increasing interest in spirituality in general, there has been a quite remarkable groundswell of interest in the Dominican path and Dominican spirituality. New books and articles have begun to appear on St Dominic, the early Friars Preachers, and their descendants in the Order, both male and female. Fresh and enthusiastic attention is being given to a number of known and less well-known Dominican saints and visionaries, to writers, artists and reformers, preachers and theologians, such as Bartolomé de las Casas, Johannes Tauler, Meister Eckhart, Catherine of Siena, Albert the Great, Humbert of Romans, Girolamo Savonarola, Martín de Porres, Thomas Aquinas, Margaret Ebner, and Beato Angelico. One almost has the sense of a vast and diverse continent which, for many years, was lost or buried under the waves, but is at last beginning to rise to the surface.

But how to explain such an apparently new 'appearing' of the tradition and, with that, the sense of manifest excitement and enthusiasm on the part of readers and researchers, as if at a new discovery? Has the Dominican tradition not been known, indeed well known, for centuries? And are we not already familiar with its most famous texts? And have these texts not been looked at again and again, and commented upon endlessly? So why, then, the excitement? Why is it that, as interested readers today of the Dominican tradition, we have the sense of coming upon an almost forgotten world of spiritual wisdom?

The simplest answer to this question is that for years the Dominican tradition had come to represent, at least in the popular mind, not so much a living spirituality, but rather an ancient, heavy, and somewhat stolid academic school of scholastic learning. But with the new interest in spirituality, and the unusual focus of attention it has afforded, a new window has opened unto the Dominican past. And it has become clear – a fact which will perhaps surprise some people – that even the emergence and development of scholasticism within the tradition did not exclude, at least not in the early centuries, a profound and radical form of Christian mysticism. The Order's two most celebrated scholastic theologians, St Thomas Aquinas and St Albert the Great, have both been accurately and tellingly described as 'mystics on campus'.[55] Aquinas' spiritual genius, in particular, has begun of late to be re-appraised. And, in this context, it is encouraging to note the appearance of books, in both

---

[55] See James A. Weisheipl O.P., *Mystic on Campus: Friar Thomas*, in *An Introduction to the Medieval Mystics of Europe*, Paul Szarmach (ed.) (New York 1984) p. 135.

English and French, with titles such as *Saint Thomas d'Aquin, maître spirituel*.[56]

The style of Aquinas's writing is markedly different from that of most of the mystical and spiritual literature with which we are familiar. Instead, for example, of using language that tends to be emotive or intensely dramatic, Aquinas is content to express his vision in a way that seems at times almost passionless. But this 'style' of Aquinas, for all its seeming detachment, conceals in fact a hidden depth of devotion, and a near obsession with truth: the passion of a mind in love with God. Later scholastic authors would, in time, try to imitate the calm, unruffled style of Aquinas, and seek to emulate his probing intellectual and scientific pursuit of truth. But often their work lacked vision, and lacked passion. Nevertheless, in recent centuries, this scholastic 'style' has come to be regarded as characteristic of the Dominican temper.

When, in the late nineteenth century, John Henry Newman was attempting in one of his essays to isolate the distinguishing character of Dominican 'education' – what perhaps, nowadays, we might call 'spirituality' – the adjective he chose was 'scientific'.[57] Newman, having first

[56] See Jean-Pierre Torrrell O.P., *Saint Thomas d'Aquin, maître spirituel* (Fribourg 1996), published in English as *St Thomas Aquinas: Spiritual Master* (Washington 2003). See also Robert Barron, *Thomas Aquinas: Spiritual Master* (New York 1996).

[57] John Henry Newman, *The Mission of St Benedict*, in *Historical Sketches*, vol. 2, (Westminster, Maryland 1970; first published 1858) p. 366.

divided the Christian tradition into three distinct periods, the ancient, the medieval, and the modern, saw each one of these as being typified by three religious Orders: the Benedictines, the Dominicans, and the Jesuits. To St Benedict, Newman assigned, as 'his discriminating badge, the element of Poetry; to St Dominic, the Scientific element; and to St Ignatius, the Practical.'[58] The badges assigned to St Benedict and St Ignatius are manifestly appropriate and are well deserved. But how accurate, when applied to St Dominic and to the Dominican Friars Preachers, is the adjective 'scientific'? The word does, of course, have the obvious merit of underlining the weight given in the Dominican tradition to study and research in the service of preaching. But 'scientific', at least at first hearing, evokes not Dominic, the man of the Gospel - *vir evangelicus* - surrounded and supported by his brethren in the task of preaching, but that later, less dynamic figure in Dominican history, the scholarly devotee of Neo-Thomism, the studious disciple of truth, working alone in his room, or in the library, surrounded by his books. So, the adjective 'scientific' expresses one aspect only - albeit an important aspect - of the Order's character and spirit. But once we become familiar with the early history of St Dominic, and begin to reflect on the lives and writings of Dominicans such as Jordan of Saxony, Henry Suso, Bartolomé de las Casas, Henri Dominique Lacordaire, Catherine of Siena, and Meister Eckhart, then I think we are compelled to set alongside Newman's term 'scientific'

[58] *ibid.*, p. 27.

other words, other adjectives, such as apostolic, exuberant, evangelical, risk-taking, mystical and robust.

That said, however, there is one important detail surrounding Newman's choice of the word 'scientific' that will help cast light on the reason for his choice. I have indicated already that the word selected by Newman points to something fundamental in Dominican spirituality, namely the weight and importance that is given to study and research. But there is an added reason – and I think a profound and telling reason – why Newman was justified in choosing the term 'scientific.' In the nineteenth century, at the time he was writing, the word enjoyed a far more open, more dynamic meaning than it possesses today. And it was a word that most people would have associated not merely with the accumulation of facts and knowledge, as is often the case in our own age, but with the pursuit of truth itself.

Regular and Irregular: The Dominican Observance

One detail often repeated about St Dominic is that before he founded the Order of Preachers, he had lived for several years as a Canon Regular at Osma. What is, however, less well known is that, for a short period, Dominic and his fellow preachers were officially constituted as a group of Canons Regular, and were generally recognized as such. How did this come about? According to the account given by Jordan of Saxony in his *Libellus*, Dominic went to Rome, and asked Pope Innocent 'to confirm ... an Order that would be and would be called an Order of Preachers.'[59] The Pope did not accede at once to this request. He asked Dominic, first of all, to choose for himself and for his brothers, 'some approved rule' of religious life. 'When all this was done, Brother Dominic was to return to the Pope to receive confirmation of all that he had asked.'[60]

On leaving Rome that first time, Dominic may well have realized, and perhaps with some alarm, that a traditional rule by itself would not allow him the scope or the freedom necessary for preaching. Nevertheless, there is no evidence to suggest that the adoption of a rule in itself represented a complete break with what St Dominic had originally intended to establish. 'As usual,' Tugwell notes, 'we do not know what Dominic thought, we only know what he did. And he did all to ensure that his brethren were good Canons, faithful to their regular life and its observances.'[61] Vicaire, for his part, argues that Dominic and his brethren adopted the canonical rule without the least hesitation: 'What they sought from it,

[59] See S. Tugwell, *Jordan of Saxony*, p. 11.

[60] *ibid.*, p. 11. Pope Innocent's response does seem, at first hearing, to be distinctly negative. But it has been argued, and I think persuasively, by Simon Tugwell that Innocent's proposal or ordination regarding a rule was made with considerable foresight in order to help Dominic and his colleagues acquire a status that would, in time, enable them to preach throughout the whole church. See S. Tugwell, 'The Genesis of the Order of Preachers - I', *Dominican Ashram*, XVI, 2 (1887) pp. 85-7.

[61] S. Tugwell, *Friars and Canons: The Earliest Dominicans*, in J. Loades (ed.) *Monastic Studies*, II (Bangor 1991) p. 203. See also S. Tugwell, 'Notes on the Life of St Dominic', AFP LXV (1995) p. 21.

through the text of Premontré, was regularity, that is to say, liturgical life – the morning chapter, Mass, the canonical hours solemnly recited in the church; ascetical life organized down to its very details in accordance with the strictest monastic tradition.'[62]

That summary is impressive, and the dependence on Premontré is clear. But Dominic and his brethren – being determined to become not only contemplatives of the Word but also active, itinerant preachers – needed something more than a life of solemn 'regularity'. So when Dominic set about drawing up the Constitutions of the Order, he did not hesitate to change, and in important ways, the received Premonstratensian model of canonical life.[63] As a result, within a few years under his leadership, the tradition of regular observance was adapted until it became a servant of 'the holy preaching'. Radical poverty had always been regarded as a key element in religious life. But St Dominic gave it a new focus. In the winter of 1219, he obtained from Rome a Bull of Commendation which made it abundantly clear that the poverty envisaged for his brothers was not that of enclosed, contemplative monks or canons but of active, itinerant preachers, an *apostolic* poverty, in other words, an asceticism of *witness* which enabled them, as free men, to 'go through the field of this world ... [casting] their seeds so that, as the Lord grants them

---

[62] M-H. Vicaire O.P., *Saint Dominic and His Times*, (Green Bay, Wisconsin 1964) pp. 208-9.

[63] See Vicaire, *St Dominic* p. 210. See also S. Tugwell, *Early Dominicans*, pp. 455-65.

increase, they can bring back their harvest to his barn with joy.'[64]

By far the most dramatic change Dominic introduced into the traditional framework of religious life was 'the law of dispensation'. With this striking and unexpected innovation proof was given by Dominic, if proof were needed, that he was determined to adapt, wherever necessary, the traditional monastic observances to the demands of preaching. In the light of this new law, those friars who needed time to study, for example, in order to preach the Word, could be dispensed even from important community functions. So the reference to dispensation (in the Prologue to the early *Constitutions*) though brief and seemingly innocuous, marks in fact a quite extraordinary change. The text reads: 'The superior is to have the right to dispense the brethren in his own community whenever it seems useful to him, particularly in things which seem likely to obstruct study or preaching or the good of souls.'[65] Clearly the preaching ministry demanded a new freedom, a new breadth of spirit. And something of that 'newness' is evident in a later sentence in the Prologue: 'to provide for the unity and peace of the whole Order, we intend and declare that our Constitu-

[64] MOPH, XXV, pp. 113-14, cited in S. Tugwell, 'Dominic the Founder - II', *Dominican Ashram*, IV, 3 (1985) p. 132. On the general question of poverty in the Order of Preachers see William A. Hinnebusch O.P., *The History of the Dominican Order: Origins and Growth to 1500* (New York 1966) pp. 145-68.

[65] *The Early Dominican Constitutions*, in S. Tugwell, *Early Dominicans*, p. 457.

tions do not bind us on pain of sin ...'[66] The reason for this declaration is explained in the Order's *Basic Constitution:* '[The] laws do not bind under sin so that the brethren may wisely embrace them "not like slaves under the law but like freemen established under grace." '[67] Dominic, as founder, was so concerned that this spirit of freedom be maintained in the Order, he was heard on one occasion to remark that if the brethren should ever be persuaded to think that failures in religious observances were sins, 'he would go himself, at that moment, through all their convents, and scratch out the rules with his knife (*et omnes regulas cum cultellino suo delere*)'![68]

Thanks to St Dominic's willingness to adapt himself both to new situations and to new demands, 'the *ordo praedicatorum* emerged in 1220 enriched by the *ordo canonicus,* not engulfed by it, and endowed with a stable canonical basis which it would probably otherwise have lacked.'[69] The *ordo praedicatorum* won out in the end. But, clearly, and for the great good of the Order, something of Dominic the Canon Regular survived in Dominic the

[66] *ibid.,* p. 457.

[67] '*Constitutio fundamentalis*', VI, *Liber constitutionum et ordinationum* (Rome 1998) p. 27. The *Basic Constitution* came into being at the General Chapter of the Order in 1968. See M-H. Vicaire, 'A Commentary on the Basic Constitution of the Friars Preachers', *Dominican Ashram* I, 1 (1982) pp. 29-44. The phrase beginning 'not like slaves' is taken from *The Rule of St Augustine,* 8.

[68] Humbert of Romans, 'Prologue XIII', in *Opera de vita regulari*, vol. II, J.J. Berthier (ed.) (Rome 1889) p. 46.

[69] S. Tugwell, *Friars and Canons*, p. 206.

preacher.[70] On this subject, Humbert of Romans, in his commentary on the *Constitutions*, says of Dominic and of the first friars that they 'took over' from the pre-existing rules and constitutions of the Canons 'everything they could find that was austere, beautiful, wise and still suited to their purposes'.[71] Those two words – 'austere' and 'beautiful' – are eloquent of one aspect of Dominican spirituality at its best. John Henry Newman, in his *Sermons Bearing on Subjects of the Day*, writes: 'Religion has two sides, a severe side, and a beautiful; and we shall be sure to swerve from the narrow way which leads to life, if we indulge ourselves in what is beautiful, while we put aside what is severe.'[72]

One of the principal monastic observances embraced with enthusiasm by Dominic and the early friars was the singing of the Divine Office in choir. But, given the demands of study and preaching, it was unthinkable that the friars, like the monks, would be able to spend the

[70] As if desiring to affirm this idea, Yves Congar noted in one of his books: 'I am convinced that there is a marked trait of the monastic spirit in the Dominican vocation ... To lose that trait would, I feel sure, be losing something of our identity as Dominicans.' See Y. Congar O.P., *Called to Life* (New York 1985) p. 3.

[71] Humbert of Romans, *Opera II*, pp. 2–3. Thomas of Cantimpré, in a wildly chauvinistic interpretation of a passage in the Book of Zechariah, declared that the name chosen for the Dominican Order – 'from all eternity' – was Beauty. 'Rope' in contrast, he proposed, was the immortal name given by God the Creator to the Franciscan Minors! See *Defense of the Mendicants* in S. Tugwell, *Early Dominicans*, p. 136.

[72] John Henry Newman, *Feasting in Captivity*, Sermon XXV, in *Sermons Bearing on Subjects of the Day* (London 1869) p. 391.

major part of their day chanting psalmody at a grave monastic pace. For that reason, in the *Primitive Constitutions*, it is clearly indicated that the liturgical office should be recited 'briefly and succinctly'.[73] Concerning this particular innovation the Dominican historian Guy Bedouelle remarks: 'The monastic tradition of the time would have found this startling.'[74] No less startling, I suspect, to the traditional (monastic) way of thinking was the bold claim of Humbert of Romans that preaching gives a clearer and more open praise of God than the Divine Office, and that 'the title "divine praise" can actually be transferred to preaching'![75]

That said, the Dominicans were not unaware that, at certain times, so eloquent of the beauty of God was the celebration of the Divine Office that it itself became a 'holy preaching'. Thus, with regard to the *Salve Regina*, for example, which the Dominicans sang every night after Compline, Jordan of Saxony remarks: 'How many people have been brought to tears of devotion by this holy praise … !'[76] And he adds that, on a number of occasions, while the brethren were singing out the line from the *Salve*, 'Turn then, most gracious advocate', one of the brothers had a vision of the mother of God. He saw her, Jordan reports, 'prostrating herself in the

[73] *Primitive Constitutions*, Distinction I, IV.

[74] Guy Bedouelle O.P., *Saint Dominic: The Grace of the Word* (San Francisco 1987) p. 108.

[75] Humbert of Romans, *Treatise*, p. 258.

[76] S. Tugwell, *Jordan of Saxony*, p. 31.

presence of her Son and praying for the safety of the whole Order.'[77]

The Dominican tradition, the focus of the present study, is a tradition to which I myself belong. And so my engagement with the subject – my enthusiasm – is inevitably that of an 'involved spectator'.[78] There might, in such a case, be a risk of highlighting only the positive aspects of the tradition, and of appearing to speak about Dominicans as if they were all saints and visionaries! But the saints themselves, within the tradition, have always been more honest and realistic. A passage in the *Dialogue* of St Catherine of Siena, for example, laments that the Dominican Order which was once 'a delightful garden' inhabited by 'men of great perfection' has been taken over by certain wretched fellows (*miseri*) who, by their disobedience, have turned the 'garden' into a wilderness.[79] This statement may well represent something

[77] *ibid.* Mary, being mother of the Word Incarnate, was regarded as a special advocate by the early Dominicans, and not least because the Order of Preachers was founded in part to defend the reality of the Incarnation. Over the centuries, Dominicans have played a key role in the development of the Marian prayer, the Rosary. See Alfonso D'Amato O.P., 'Devozione particulari', in *Il Progetto di san Domenico* (Bologna 1994) pp. 82-7; Guy Bedouelle O.P. and Alain Quilici O.P. (eds), *La bienheureuse Vierge Marie, mère des prêcheurs*, in *Les Frères prêcheurs autrement dits Dominicains* (Paris 1997) pp. 215-24; Bogus-law Kochaniewicz O.P., 'The Contribution of the Dominicans to the Development of the Rosary', *Angelicum* 81, 2 (2004) pp. 377-403.

[78] A phrase of the French philosopher, Raymond Aron, cited in Guy Bedouelle O.P., 'The Dominican Identity', *Dominican Ashram* IX, 3 (1990) p. 131.

[79] *Il Dialogo*, 158, p. 462.

of an exaggeration. But, in the *Divina Commedia* of Dante, we find similar complaints being made about the Order.[80] Thus, only a small minority of Dominicans, we're told, stay close to the original spirit of their founder, but the majority go wandering off on their own into 'wild pastures' further and further away from Dominic.

Clearly the Order has known both troughs and peaks in its long history, some of them unhappy and dark and some outstanding and inspired.[81] John Henry Newman, writing in 1846, was manifestly drawn to the Dominican ideal but, unfortunately, at that particular moment in England, the Order was not in a healthy state. Newman wrote: 'If indeed we could be Dominicans *teaching*, it were well. Meanwhile I am doubting whether the Dominicans have preserved their traditions - whether it is not a great

[80] *Paradiso*, canto XI, lines 24-9. See *The Divine Comedy: Paradiso*, (Oxford 1971) pp. 168-9.

[81] One of the saddest 'troughs' was, without question, the Dominican involvement in the Inquisition. This fact was openly acknowledged in *The Acts of the General Chapter* of the Dominican Order in 1998. In the section on the Order's mission (no.83) we read: 'The Order of Preachers regretfully remembers the role of some members of the Order in the injustices of the Inquisition.' At the suggestion of the Chapter an international seminar on the subject of the Inquisition was held a few years later in Rome. See A. Bernal Palacios O.P. (ed.), *Praedicatores inquisatores - I, The Dominicans and the Medieval Inquisition; Acts of the 1st International Seminar on the Dominicans and the Inquisition, 23-25 February 2002, Dissertationes Historicae,* XXIX (Rome 2004). It should be noted that the role played by Dominicans in the Inquisition has at times been greatly exaggerated. See Guy Bedouelle, *Saint Dominic: The Grace of the Word* (San Francisco 1987) pp. 183-92.

idea extinct.'[82] Even as Newman was writing these words, the Order was already, in fact, undergoing a revival in France, led and inspired by Henri Dominique Lacordaire. And, in England itself, within no more than a generation or two, the Order was set to enjoy an unexpected recovery, something which Newman could never have foreseen.

That capacity somehow to recover or re-discover the original spirit of the Order, at a time when all seemed lost, is one of the remarkable aspects of Dominican history. And no less remarkable is the fact that, unlike the great Franciscan and Carmelite Orders which, in the course of their history, split into different branches and congregations, the Dominican Order has always managed to preserve its institutional unity. What has kept the brethren together, over the centuries, is no doubt a combination of many factors. One, for example, is the great system of democracy, bestowed on the Order by St Dominic at the beginning; also the spirit of freedom and fraternity he enshrined in the Order's *Primitive Constitutions*, the traits of beauty and austerity inherited from the Canons Regular, and the desire to defend truth and the

---

[82] Letter to J.D. Dalgairns, July 6, 1846, in *The Letters and Diaries of John Henry Newman*, XI, C.S. Dessain (ed.) (London 1961) p. 195. In another letter to Dalgairns (July 21, 1846), although expressing once again his fear that 'the Dominicans have lost their tradition', Newman nevertheless admits: 'The idea I like exceedingly.' *ibid.*, p. 212. And one month later he remarked: 'My present feeling is that what the world, or at least England, wants as much as anything, is Dominicans.' Letter to T.T. Fox, August 20, 1846, p. 227.

love of learning. These things define the spirit of the Order. They are tangible and clear, and as long as the Order survives, they will be recognised as forming a necessary part of its identity.[83]

But there are other factors, less tangible though no less important, and some of these I have attempted to name in this chapter, and in the chapters which follow. It should, however, be noted here that, generally speaking, Dominicans tend to be nervous about any attempt to sum up with absolute precision or to fix in stone, as it were, the nature of their spirituality. Because it is a preacher's vocation, the Dominican vocation is, in its essence, a *dynamic* vocation. It is shaped, therefore, not only by its own pre-established laws and constitutions, but by the demands of history and the needs of the hour. And thus, in contrast to a life of monastic enclosure, it has the right and even the duty not to be always consistent or predictable in its activity. Even in its most authentic forms and expressions there will always, in the end, be something elusive about Dominican spirituality, something which one might even call 'irregular'. For, in the

[83] For an understanding of how Dominican spirituality draws its life from the Order's Constitutions and system of government, see Timothy Radcliffe O.P., *Freedom and Responsibility: Towards a Spirituality of Government [Letter to the Dominican Order]*, in *Sing a New Song: The Christian Vocation* (Dublin 1999) pp. 82-120; Carlos Alfonso Aspiroz Costa O.P., 'Libertad y responsabilidad dominicanas: Hacia una espiritualidad del gobierno', *Angelicum* 81, 2 (2004) pp. 431-44; Malachy Dwyer O.P., 'Reclaiming the Dominican Vision for the 21st Century: Pursuing Communion in Government, Role of Community Chapter', *Dominican Ashram* XV, 2 (1996) pp. 78-89.

43

preacher's life, the pattern of religious observance is never static or fixed, but always forms part of a life lived in response to the needs of others and to the demands of the Gospel at any given moment. It is, in short, in the thoughtful and revelatory phrase of Blessed Jordan of Saxony, an '*apostolic* observance'.[84]

---

[84] The phrase occurs in a prayer addressed to St Dominic, which may well have been composed, according to Vicaire, around the time of Dominic's canonization. See M-H. Vicaire O.P., *Saint Dominic and His Times* (Green Bay, Wisconsin 1964) pp. 394 and 530. Italics added. The Latin is '*apostolicae religioni*', which Vicaire renders correctly as 'l'observance apostolique'.

2

Dominicans and Happiness

To begin to understand a particular tradition or spirituality, it is enough sometimes to take hold of a single word common to that tradition – in this case a word such as 'truth', for example, or 'democracy' or 'contemplation' or 'preaching' – and hold on to that word as you would hold on to a piece of string to see how far it leads. The word I want to suggest that we examine, in this chapter, is not perhaps an obvious choice. But it is a word which can, I am convinced, take us no small distance in our understanding of Dominican life and Dominican spirituality. It is the word 'happiness'.

Blaise Pascal, the French Catholic philosopher, was overheard to remark on one occasion that, 'Nobody is as happy as a real Christian.' The statement is encouraging certainly, but its validity stands or falls by that small word 'real'. For how many of us, in practice, attain to the happiness of which Pascal speaks? The German philosopher, Friedrich Nietzsche – no friend to the Christian gospel, but well aware, all the same, of its most important claims - remarked once on the impact of Christ on human history: 'His disciples,' he said, 'should look more redeemed'![1]

Involvement in religion or in the pursuit of a spiritual life is such a serious matter, believers in all religions have a tendency to become very grim, solemn people. And Christianity is no exception. Laughter and happiness can come to be regarded as somehow frivolous and even as subversive of an authentic moral and spiritual way of life. 'Sometimes people, even Catholics,' Vincent McNabb writes, 'are frightened away from the spiritual life. They think it aims at making us miserable.'[2] But McNabb himself when, as a young man, he entered the Dominican Order, began immediately to breathe in an atmosphere that was altogether different. 'I was immensely surprised and delighted,' he tells us, 'to find that sadness was never considered one of the products of the religious life ... if you hadn't joy, out you went!'[3]

My intention in this chapter is, first of all, to examine the theme of happiness as it emerged in some of the very early stories concerning the Friars Preachers; second, the theme as it was developed in a number of Dominican mystical texts; and finally, the theme as it was taken up and reflected upon in the writings of St Thomas Aquinas.

[1] Cited in Paul Tillich, *The Boundaries of our Being* (London 1973) p. 256.
[2] Vincent McNabb, O.P., *The Craft of Suffering* (London 1936) p. 38.
[3] *ibid.*, p. 38.

1. A Vision of Gospel Joy

(a) *Laughter in* The Lives of the Brethren

Of all the early friars, perhaps the most spontaneously good-humoured and exuberant was Blessed Jordan of Saxony, Dominic's first successor as Master. Almost an entire section of the *Vitae Fratrum* is devoted to a number of his witty replies.[4] Everyone, we're told, longed to hear him. And he attracted an enormous number of vocations to the Order. Once, in 1229, when he was on his way to Genoa, bringing with him a batch of new Dominicans, one of the group, during night prayer or Compline, started laughing, and then all the rest joined in 'right merrily'.[5] A senior brother reprimanded them at once, and by using signs, ordered them to stop. But this 'only set them off laughing more than ever'. As soon as Compline was over, Jordan turned to the friar in question, and said: 'Brother, who made you their master? What right have you to take them to task?' Then, addressing the other brothers, Jordan said: 'Laugh to your hearts' content ... and don't stop on that man's account. You have my full leave, and it is only right that you should

---

[4] Gerald de Frachet, *Vitae Fratrum,* III, 42, MOPH I, B.M. Reichert (ed.) (Louvain 1896), pp. 137–46.

[5] *Vitae Fratrum,* III, 42, xvii, p. 144; trans., Placid Conway in *Lives of the Brethren* (London 1955) p. 127.

laugh after breaking from the devil's thraldom ... Laugh on, then, and be as merry as you please.'[6]

This little episode from the *Vitae Fratrum* might seem naive and inconsequential. But it serves to underline something really fundamental about the early Dominicans and their fresh grasp of the Gospel. Throughout the preaching ministry of Dominic, a vision of Gospel joy had come to define itself over against some very grim and very gloomy notions indeed. So Jordan of Saxony's instinctive refusal here to silence the brothers' laughter was very probably, I would say, no accident.

That the early Dominicans should go to the trouble of preserving a story of this kind is really quite remarkable, especially in view of the prevailing medieval attitude to laughter. St Benedict, in his Rule, had explicitly forbidden 'talk leading to laughter'. 'Only a fool,' he observed, quoting Ecclesisticus 21:2, 'raises his voice in laughter.'[7] What St Benedict is attacking here is, presumably, that boisterous laughter which prevents the monk from really listening. For there is a kind of hilarity which is little more than a way of avoiding one's own guilt or fear by mocking the weaknesses and disabilities of others. Nevertheless, the fact remains that laughter can also build up,

[6] *Vitae Fratrum*, III, 42, xvii, pp. 144-5; Conway, *Lives*, p. 127. Striking in itself, Jordan's defence of the brothers' laughter is all the more striking when one remembers that, in line with the general monastic tradition, such rowdy behaviour in choir and elsewhere was characterized in the *Primitive Constitutions* of the Friars Preachers as a fault, albeit as one of the minor faults (Dist.I, XXI.).

[7] *The Rule of St Benedict*, Timothy Fry, O.S.B. (ed.) (Collegeville 1981) VII, p. 201.

encourage and set free. For those who are 'pure of heart,' as Josef Pieper reminds us, 'can laugh in a freedom that creates freedom in others.'[8]

Happily, then, we don't have to agree with the rather grim conclusion, expressed in an article I read some time ago, entitled 'Get Serious! The Monastic Condemnation of Laughter'. In this article the author writes: 'At the best of times, laughter is a movement toward the surface, toward the shallows. It is always escapist. It is always a distraction because it is always a movement away from the quiet centre of one's being.'[9] Now, that statement, in spite of possessing the dubious merit of sounding very 'spiritual' is not, I would suggest, very wise. The deep, almost uncontrollable laughter which springs from Gospel joy, far from being something that is unspiritual or shallow or escapist is, in fact, simply an ecstasy of the inner heart, a saving 'movement' away from the preciosity of cold self-love, an impulse of surrender and delight towards the neighbour and towards God. Unfortunately, however, we tend to take ourselves far too seriously, as G.K. Chesterton constantly reminds us. '[S]olemnity,' he writes, 'flows out of men naturally; but laughter is a leap. It is easy to be heavy: hard to be light. Satan fell by the force of gravity.'[10]

---

[8] Josef Pieper, *A Brief Reader on the Virtues of the Human Heart* (San Francisco 1991) p. 44.

[9] Kenneth C. Russell, 'Get Serious! The Monastic Condemnation of Laughter', *Review for Religious* (May-June 1993) p. 376. This one unfortunate statement apart, Russell's paper makes interesting reading.

[10] G.K. Chesterton, *Orthodoxy,* in *Collected Works,* vol. I, D. Dooley (ed.) (San Francisco 1986) p. 326.

And again: 'In perfect force there is a kind of frivolity, an airiness that can maintain itself in the air ... a characteristic of the great saints is their power of levity. Angels can fly because they can take themselves lightly.'[11]

(b) The Joy of Dominic and the Early Dominicans

St Dominic was called 'vir evangelicus'.[12] The one passion of his life was to preach a truth he could not keep to himself. And he preached it by word and by example. But also – to a remarkable degree – he preached it by joy. '[H]is face was always radiant,' we are told, and '[B]y his cheerfulness he easily won the love of everybody. Without difficulty he found his way into peoples' hearts as soon as they saw him.'[13] Cecilia tells us that '[A] kind of radiance shone from his forehead and between his eyebrows, which drew everyone to venerate and love him. He always appeared cheerful and happy.'[14]

On one occasion, noticing that one of his own companions, a certain Brother Bertrand, was weeping too much over his sins, and 'tormenting himself excessively',[15] Dominic decided to intervene. He commanded Bertrand

[11] ibid., p. 325.

[12] Jordan of Saxony, Libellus de principiis Ordinis Praedicatorum, MOPH, XVI, no.104, p. 75.

[13] ibid., nos.103-4, p. 74; translated by S. Tugwell in Jordan of Saxony: On the Beginnings of the Friars Preachers (Dublin 1982) p. 26.

[14] Blessed Cecilia, Miracula, 15. See V. Koudelka, Dominic (London 1997) p. 56.

[15] Vitae Fratrum, II, 19, p. 80; translated by S. Tugwell in Early Dominicans: Selected Writings (New York 1982) p. 91.

'not to weep for his own sins, but for those of others'. And 'his words had such a powerful effect', we're told, 'that thereafter Bertrand wept profusely for others, but was unable to weep for himself even when he wanted to'![16]

In another early text concerning Dominic, a great burst of laughter is recorded. What provoked the laughter was an unusual miracle he worked in the Church of St Sixtus. According to the ancient account, Dominic, with un-restrained enthusiasm, unmasked the Evil One who had come flying into the Church disguised as a bird in order to prevent him preaching. All the Dominicans who were present, both the brethren and the sisters, at once burst out laughing (*subridentibus fratribus et sororibus*).[17] Although many saints, over the centuries, have worked miracles which have moved crowds of people to wonder and amazement, in all of Christian hagiography, I have never heard of a miracle which provoked immediate and joyous laughter among those present. Cecilia, in her *Legenda*, refers to it as '*iocundum miraculum*', 'a laughter-stirring miracle'.[18]

Something of the same surprise of joy pervades *The Dialogue* of St Catherine of Siena. At one point, Catherine is informed by God the Father that the Dominican Order is 'in itself ... wholly delightful'.[19] Dominic, he tells her,

---

[16] *ibid.*, p. 42.

[17] Blessed Cecilia, *Miracula*, 10. See AFP, XXXVII (1967) p. 37.

[18] *ibid.*, p. 38. See also *The Legend of St Dominic by Blessed Cecilia*, in Conway, *Lives*, p. 86.

[19] St Catherine of Siena, *The Dialogue*, 158, trans., S. Noffke O.P. (New York 1980) p. 339.

built his 'ship' both 'very spacious' and also 'very happy'. What is more, the Order, he declares, is not tied 'to the guilt of deadly sin'. So 'both the perfect and the not-so-perfect fare well on this ship'![20]

A no less enthusiastic statement concerning the Order founded by Dominic occurs in a letter composed by Jordan of Saxony. Just over 50 of Jordan's letters have survived, and the word 'joy' occurs on almost every page. Most of these letters were sent by Jordan to his beloved Dominican friend, the enclosed contemplative, Diana d'Andalò. In one letter, addressed not to Diana only but to her entire community at Bologna, Jordan quotes a phrase from Matthew's Gospel about joy: 'Enter into the joy of your Lord' (Mt. 25:21). The meaning of the phrase is clear enough. But Jordan, in a moment of sheer Dominican bravado and enthusiasm, decides – for the space of a paragraph – to change or to extend its meaning. For him 'the joy of the Lord' has somehow become one thing with the happiness of belonging to the Order of Preachers. And so he says 'Enter into the joy of your Lord' meaning by 'Lord' that form of the grace of the Lord which is the Order itself. Enter into it, Jordan says, into that life of obedient communion, and 'all your sorrow shall be turned into joy, and your joy no-one can take from you'![21]

[20] *ibid.*, 158, pp. 338–9.
[21] *To Heaven with Diana: A Study of Jordan of Saxony and Diana d'Andalò with a translation of the Letters of Jordan*, Gerald Vann O.P. (ed. and trans.) (London 1960) p. 80.

On the subject of joy, there is one remarkable text composed by the enclosed Dominican contemplative Margaret Ebner, in which we are told about a Dominican nun in her community who, although she was within days of death, had clearly already entered into the joy of her Lord. Margaret writes: 'At this time one of our sisters lay dying. She had served God earnestly in suffering and poverty. And since she had already lain four days without eating I went to her and told her I noticed that *she wanted to go to God before me.*'[22] That last, unexpected statement must surely have been accompanied by a look or smile of irony. Our saint, the Blessed Margaret, was clearly possessed of a somewhat dry sense of humour! But what response, then, did the dying nun make to Margaret's words?

> Then she clapped her hands together for joy and laughed so that it was heard everywhere in the room. One of the sisters said to her, 'You are acting like someone who has just come from a wedding.' Then I replied, 'You act like someone who wants to go to a wedding.' Then she laughed so loudly that I noticed that God had granted her special grace. She assured me that this was true, and at that I laughed like her and was so happy that I could not sleep that night because of the joy in my heart over the eternal joy for which she longed.[23]

Further indications of Dominican joy are evident in a story from the *Vitae Fratrum* which concerns a certain Peter of Aubenas. Peter had originally intended to join the Friars Preachers. But, when he made the acquaintance of

[22] *Margaret Ebner: Major Works*, Leonard P. Hindsley, O.P. (ed.) (New York 1993) p. 148. Italics added.
[23] *ibid.*

a notably austere group of men called the Waldensians, he was at once confused about what to do. As the text puts it, Peter 'saw in them [the Waldensians] more outward signs of humility and of the virtues of piety, while he considered the friars too cheerful and showy' (*iocundos et ... pomposos*).[24] In an anguish of indecision, Peter begged God 'to reveal to him, in his mercy, what he ought to do in this dilemma'. Well, he got his answer, but in a dream. The text says: 'he imagined that he was walking along a road with a dark wood on the left side of it, in which he saw the Waldensians all going their separate ways, with sad, solemn faces.' But, on the other side of the road, after walking for some time beside a very beautiful high wall, he 'at last came to a gate'. When he looked in through the gate, he saw, in contrast to the dark, solemn wood, 'an exquisite meadow, planted with trees and colourful with flowers'. In the meadow, 'he saw a crowd of Friars Preachers in a ring, with joyful faces raised towards heaven'. And he saw that 'one of them was holding the Body of Christ in his upraised hands'. Peter was overwhelmed. The text says that, when he woke up, he 'found himself bathed in tears ... his heart joyful'. The path was now clear in front of him. Within a few days, he had joined the Dominican Order, and we read that 'he ran his course in the Order happily to its end'.[25]

Even allowing for a certain Dominican chauvinism in the telling of this story, one thing can be said at once about the early Friars Preachers: they certainly looked

[24] See S. Tugwell, *Early Dominicans*, p. 138.
[25] *ibid.*, p. 138.

'redeemed'. No objections on that score, I should imagine – even from Friedrich Nietzsche! But it is significant all the same that Peter was so deeply troubled at first by the friars' manifest joy. Holiness of life had somehow come to be associated with bowed heads and sad faces. And these God-shaken, active Dominicans looked far 'too cheerful'!

(c) Living the Beatitudes

Radiance, happiness, cheerfulness, joy. Fine words, all of them, and fine qualities. But how relevant to our situation today are these examples of medieval cheerfulness? In the present age we are living through a period of history when, aided by the media, we have become perhaps more aware than at any other time in history of the great distress of people in every part of the world. 'What kind of times are these,' exclaims the German poet, Bertold Brecht, 'when to talk about trees/Is almost a crime because it implies silence/About so many horrors?' ('To Those Born Later'). The question is rhetorical, but it demands, if not immediate answers, then at least some sort of honest and serious reflection. With reference to Dominic's joy, what is important to note first of all is that, in the preacher's spirit, there was never anything of cold indifference to the needs of others. 'He always appeared cheerful and happy,' we read in the *Miracula* of Cecilia, except, that is, 'when he was moved by compassion for any trouble which was affecting his neighbour'.[26]

---

[26] Blessed Cecilia, *Miracula*, 15. See V. Koudelka, *Dominic*, p. 56.

When, for the first time, we come upon some of these stories about the early brethren, and their joy, we might be inclined to think that they were happy simply because they were 'having a good time'. Now I have no doubt that they did, on occasion, enjoy themselves enormously. They certainly seem to have enjoyed preaching.[27] When one of the early friars famous for preaching, Reginald of Orleans, was asked: 'Do you ever feel depressed, Master, that you have put on our habit?' he replied: 'I very much doubt if there is any merit in it for me, because I have always found so much pleasure in the Order'![28] So the Friars Preachers were manifestly happy people. But the springs of their joy came from a source much deeper, I suspect, than that of any ordinary delight or simple pleasure.

Even a brief familiarity with early Dominican sources makes it clear that life in the Order was far from easy in those first years. Thomas of Cantimpré, for example, commenting on the difficulty of the Friars Preachers' life, writes: 'I could not sustain such discomfort for even a single day.' And he adds: 'The friars are tormented by work, distracted by all kinds of different business, and yet

---

[27] This fact is evident from a comment made by an anonymous Dominican writing in Paris in the thirteenth century: 'Scripture,' he says, 'is difficult to understand, but preaching is easy and delightful.' See *Expositio super Apocalypsim*, edited under the name of Thomas Aquinas in *Opera omnia, Opuscula alia dubia*, vol. I (Parma 1868) p. 410. This text was written by one of an équipe working at St Jacques between 1240 and 1244.

[28] See *Jordan of Saxony: On the Beginnings of the Friars Preachers*, p. 16.

they survive unbroken.'[29] In similar vein, Jordan of
Saxony writes to Diana: 'Here on earth we are wounded
every day and our hearts are torn to shreds; and every day
our miseries cause us to cry out, Who shall deliver us
from the body of this death?' But Jordan goes on at once
to say: 'these things we must bear with patience and, so
far as our daily work allows, dwell in mind and heart with
him who alone can deliver us from our distresses …
Meanwhile then let us accept with joy whatever sad
things may come to us.'[30] Not just acceptance is
mentioned here by Jordan, but acceptance 'with joy.'
Jordan was obviously someone who had deeply absorbed
the wisdom of the Beatitudes. Writing to Diana, on one
occasion, he speaks of 'that poverty of spirit which gives
you the kingdom of heaven'. And he adds: 'I do not say
which will give you the kingdom: it gives it to you here
and now; your Bridegroom himself tells us, Happy are the
poor in spirit for theirs is the kingdom of heaven.'[31]

[29] Thomas of Cantimoré, *Defense of the Mendicants*, in S. Tugwell,
Early Dominicans, p. 133.

[30] G. Vann, *To Heaven with Diana*, p. 139. A Franciscan friar, whom
Jordan met when he was in England, was suffering so much from gout
in the foot he was laid up for two years. Jordan wrote to the poor man
with both warmth of compassion and sharpness of wit: 'Brother, do
not be ashamed though the Father of our Lord Jesus Christ is drawing
you to Himself *by the foot*'! See Thomas of Eccleston, *De adventu
Fratrum Minorum in Angliam*, cited in A.G. Little, 'Three Sermons of
Friar Jordan of Saxony, the Successor of St Dominic, preached in
England, A.D 1229', *The English Historical Review*, CCXIII (1939) p. 6.
Italics added.

[31] *ibid.*, p. 70.

Jordan of Saxony was not the first Dominican to learn the secret of happiness from the wisdom he found contained in the Beatitudes. Significantly, in a prayer attributed to Dominic himself in the *Nine Ways of Prayer* [of St Dominic], there is a statement on the subject, which is unusually striking. In this prayer, Dominic, without the least hesitation, asks God for 'delight and enjoyment' both for himself and for his brethren.[32] But what Dominic aspires to in this prayer is not some kind of wilful heartiness, but rather, as he explains, 'delight and enjoyment in *putting the Beatitudes into practice*' - an evangelical joy, in other words, a happiness so deeply grounded in supernatural faith and hope that even 'in the most profound poverty, in bitter grief, in severe persecution, in great hunger and thirst for righteousness, in all the cares and worries of mercy', even in these circumstances, each individual brother would, in St Dominic's words, 'consider himself blessed'.[33] One of the saint's early companions, Brother Buonviso, tells us that even when he was 'badly treated' Dominic did not become angry or depressed but 'showed all the signs of being particularly pleased'![34]

Among the many different examples recorded in the *Vitae Fratrum* of the brethren's 'delight and enjoyment in putting the Beatitudes into practice', by far the most vivid to my mind and, in a sense, the most outrageous, involves

[32] *The Nine Ways of Prayer*, in S. Tugwell, *Early Dominicans*, p. 99.

[33] *ibid.*, pp. 99-100. Italics added.

[34] 'The Testimony of Brother Buonviso', *Canonization Process of St Dominic*, 22. See S. Tugwell, *Early Dominicans*, p. 72.

yet again that exuberant man of joy, Blessed Jordan of
Saxony. Here is the story taken direct from the *Vitae*:

> In company with a batch of our brethren, one morning the
> blessed father sent them all out into the town to beg bread
> for their breakfast, bidding them to join him at a
> neighbouring fountain. When they met again they found
> they had scarcely enough for half their number. Then the
> Master, breaking forth into joyful strains of the praises of
> God, exhorted the others by word and by example to do the
> same, and presently they were all filled with such spiritual
> gladness and holy joy that a woman standing by took
> scandal at the sight, and rebuked them – 'Are you not all
> religious men? Whence comes it that you are merry-making
> at this early hour?' But when she learnt the real cause of
> their mirth, and saw them rejoicing over their want of food,
> she was deeply touched, and hurrying home brought them
> bread and wine and cheese, saying: 'If you were merry and
> gave thanks to God for such a miserable pittance, I want you
> now to have greater cause for rejoicing.' After this she
> withdrew feeling highly edified, and begged for a remem-
> brance in their prayers.[35]

2. Expansive Joy: The Rhineland Mystics

(a) 'Into the Open': Eckhart and Suso

'Happy are those who suffer for righteousness' sake.' This
phrase from the Beatitudes is quoted by Meister Eckhart
in a passage in which he faces head-on the seeming

---

[35] *Vitae Fratrum*, III, 34, p. 127; translated by Conway, *Lives*, p. 113.

contradiction in Christ's words about persecution and happiness.[36] For how can happiness be concomitant with human misery and suffering? Eckhart explains that Jesus' command to take up our cross is 'not merely a commandment, as it is commonly said and thought: it is a promise and a divine prescription for a man to make all his suffering, all his deeds, and all his life happy and joyful. It is more a reward than a commandment'. According to Eckhart, 'whoever has abandoned self and completely gone forth from self, for him nothing could be a cross or pain or suffering: it would all be a joy.'[37]

But why pain and suffering in the first place? Why are they necessary? Why the 'narrow path'? There is, as we well know, no simple answer to this question. But Eckhart is concerned to make at least one thing clear. 'It is not due to God's justice, or his severity, that he demands so much of us, rather it comes from his great bounty, for he wants the soul to be capacious so as to hold the largesse he is ready to bestow.'[38] Eckhart admits that this teaching about the narrow path 'sounds hard and a great matter ... But when one has got into it, no life is easier, more delightful or lovelier.'[39] And he says further: 'God is always ready, but we are unready. God is near us, but we

[36] *The Book of Divine Comfort*, in *Meister Eckhart: Sermons and Treatises*, vol. III, M. O'C. Walshe (ed.) (Longmead 1987) p. 89.

[37] *ibid.*, p. 89.

[38] Sermon 69, in *Meister Eckhart: Sermons and Treatises*, vol. II [German Sermons and Treatises], M.O'C. Walshe (ed.) (Longmeads 1981) p. 169.

[39] *ibid.*, p. 49.

are far from him ... The prophet says: "God leads the just through narrow paths to the highway that they may come out into the open".'[40]

'Into the open' is a wonderful phrase and an accurate one. It recalls that aspect of spiritual life or experience which Dominican contemplatives sometimes call 'expansion'. St Thomas, in his commentary on Psalm 34, speaks of a joy which is nothing less than 'an expansion of the heart' (latitudinem cordis), a joy so full 'it breaks forth externally from within'.[41] Margaret Ebner, the Dominican nun and mystic, describes for us how, on certain occasions, when she received Christ in the Eucharist: 'my heart was so full that I could not comprehend it. I thought it was as wide as the whole world.'[42] Blessed Henry Suso, in his book The Life of the Servant, recounts a similar kind of experience. Once, when praying the Sursum Corda before the Canon of the Mass, he found himself being lifted up in meditation into God. But, at that same moment, his heart expanded to include every living thing on earth and in heaven. 'Through me,' he says, 'all creatures were also raised up.'[43] And he says further:

I contemplated in my inner eye myself, and with all that I am, body and soul, and all my powers, and placed around

[40] ibid., p. 50.

[41] St Thomas Aquinas, Postilla super Psalmos, 34, in Expositio in aliquot libros Veteris Testamenti, in Opera omnia, vol. XIV (Parma 1863) p. 276.

[42] Margaret Ebner, p. 89.

[43] Henry Suso, The Life of the Servant, trans., J.M. Clark (London 1952) p. 35.

myself all the creatures that God ever created in heaven, on earth and in the four elements, each with its own particular name, whether it be bird of the air, beast of the forest, fish in the water, leaf and grass of the earth, the countless grains of sand on the sea shore, and moreover, all the tiny drops of water which have ever fallen or still fall as dew, or snow, or rain. I wished that each of them might resound in a sweet instrument, tuned to the innermost melody of my heart and that they may thus be played as a new joyous hymn of praise to my beloved gentle Lord from eternity to eternity. Then the loving arms of the soul stretched out and extended themselves rejoicingly towards the countless numbers of all these creatures. It was [my soul's] endeavour to fill them all with zeal, just as a fresh joyous precentor urges the choir to sing joyfully with him and to raise up their hearts to God, singing 'Lift up your hearts.'[44]

After this first meditation Suso opened his mind and heart in prayer to all his fellow human beings on earth, both saints and sinners:

I contemplate my heart and the hearts of all men and women, considering what pleasure and joy, love and peace those taste who give their hearts to God alone, and on the other hand, what injury and suffering, pain and unrest transitory love inflicts on its slaves. Then I called out with great desire to my heart and all other hearts wherever they may be, to all the ends of the earth: 'Come, imprisoned hearts, come away from the narrow bonds of transient love! ... Raise yourselves up to freedom and return to the loving God. Lift up your hearts!'[45]

[44] ibid., pp. 35-6.
[45] ibid., p. 36.

(b) 'God Makes Merry': A Dominican Theology

The gift of expansive joy which Suso describes here so powerfully is nothing less than a participation in the joy of God. But it is not Suso, but Eckhart – Suso's spiritual master – who, more than any other Dominican I can think of, delights in ringing the changes on the mystery of God's joy. Here he is in characteristic form: 'Now I shall say what I never said before. God enjoys himself. His own enjoyment is such that it includes his enjoyment of all creatures.'[46] And again, from another homily: 'God is so joyful ... he completely pours out his nature ... In the same way, if one were to let a horse run about in a green meadow ... it would be the horse's nature to pour forth its whole strength in leaping about in the meadow ... In the same way, it is a joy to God and a satisfaction to him ... to pour out his nature and his being completely.'[47] The image is a remarkable one, both daring and illuminating. And no less daring is Eckhart's intuition of what he calls 'laughter' at the very heart of the Trinity: 'the Father laughs at the Son and the Son at the Father, and the laughing brings forth pleasure, and the pleasure brings forth joy, and the joy brings forth love.'[48]

[46] Sermon 27: *Nolite timere eos*, in *Meister Eckhart: A Modern Translation*, trans., R.B. Blakney (New York 1941) p. 225.

[47] *Meister Eckhart: An Introduction to his Works with an Anthology of His Sermons*, trans., J.M. Clark (London 1957) p. 226.

[48] Sermon 18: *Scio hominem in Christo ante annos quatordecim*, in F. Pfeiffer (ed.), *Meister Eckhart, Deutsche Mystiker des Mittelalters* Bd.2 (Leipzig 1857; repr. Scientia Verlag, Aalen, 1962). I am grateful to Oliver Davies for translating this fragment from Sermon 18 at my

One of the most delightful and moving of all Eckhart's images occurs in a short treatise he wrote concerned with progress in the spiritual life. In the first stage, Eckhart tells us, the inner or new man is like a small child: 'he still staggers from chair to chair and leans against the walls and still feeds himself on milk.'[49] But, in the second stage, the inner man begins to grow up: 'he turns his back on humanity and his face to God, creeps out of his mother's lap and laughs up at his heavenly Father'![50] According to Eckhart 'the higher each saint is the greater his joy'. And the same holds true for the angels. 'Yet all their joy combined is as small as a lentil compared with the joy that God has at that act. For God makes merry and laughs [at the sight of] good deeds'![51]

Cont.

request. On the subject of laughter, the Dominican contemplative Margaret Ebner describes a dream-vision in which, to her great surprise, she encounters the 'Child Jesus laughing' and then afterwards exclaiming, 'Has not all that I have told you come true?' See *Margaret Ebner*, p. 145.

[49] *The Book of Benedictus: Of the Nobleman*, in *Meister Eckhart: The Essential Sermons*, trans. E. Colledge and B. McGinn (London 1981) p. 241.

[50] *ibid.*, p. 242.

[51] *Meister Eckhart: Sermons and Treatises* vol. 2, p. 305. Worth noting here is a statement concerning God's joy in us by the Dominican Vincent McNabb: 'When our heart is a home of prayer. God is so much at home with us that all the Blessed Trinity are there, too. They break bread with us and make merry; and we, too, make merry, with the merry-making of God within us.' See V. McNabb O.P., *The Craft of Prayer* (London 1935) p. 13.

These radiant lines from Eckhart call to mind a short, remarkable sentence concerning laughter which the medieval contemplative, Mechtild of Magdeburg, heard the Lord addressing to her on one occasion. Mechtild admits that, up to a certain stage in her life, she had considered laughing not only frivolous but 'wrong'.[52] What changed Mechtild's mind on the subject was a vision she received once on the feast of St Dominic. The Lord explained to her, first of all, that Dominic was a great example of moderation, that he never troubled his fellow Dominicans 'with things arising from some whim of his own' and that, in fact, 'he often improved the food to help and show affection for his brethren, so that the young brothers might not think back on the world and so that the older ones might not succumb on the way.'[53] But then, addressing directly the subject of laughter, the Lord added, and the sentence is memorable, 'whenever Dominic laughed, he did so with the true delight of the Holy Spirit.'[54]

These statements are certainly remarkable. But, as we listen to the voices of Mechtild and Eckhart, it might well be that we begin to hear within us another voice, a sceptical voice, which says: 'Yes - that's fine for the saints and the angels, but it's too high a conversation for me.'

---

[52] *The Flowing Light of the Godhead*, trans., F. Tobin (New York 1998) p. 165. Mechtild (c.1207-c.1282) was for many years closely associated with Dominicans, but she ended her life as a Cistercian in the monastery of Helfta.

[53] *ibid.*, p. 165.

[54] *ibid.*, p. 165.

But Eckhart, true master that he is, and true Dominican, will not for an instant let us slip away with that little thought. 'This joy,' he insists, 'is near you, it is in you! There is no one among you whose spirit is so base, whose mind is so weak, no one so far away from God, as not to be able to find this joy within himself ... and find it before leaving this Church, and even in this instant to perceive it while I am still preaching! He can find it, live it and have it within himself as truly as God is God and I am a man.'[55]

3. The Joy of Aquinas

'O happy teacher' is a phrase used a number of times by Bernard Gui in his life of St Thomas: 'O happy teacher, who lived according to the doctrine you taught, reckoning earthly things as nothing compared with the foretasted joy of heaven!'[56] This wisdom and this joy Thomas shared almost compulsively with others. In his biography, Gui notes that 'his goodness to others had a sort of quick spontaneous alacrity which, in a way, paralleled the divine outpouring of his doctrine'.[57]

Many of the texts in Gui concerning Thomas remind one of St Dominic. Once, for example, when Thomas was preaching during Holy Week in Rome, he succeeded, we are told, in 'moving his hearers to tears; and the next day,

---

[55] Sermon 66: *Euge, serve bone et fidelis*, in *Maître Eckhart: Traites et sermons*, trans., A. de Libera (Paris 1993) p. 358.

[56] *The Life of St Thomas Aquinas: Biographical Documents*, K. Foster O.P. (ed.) (London 1959) p. 53. See also pp. 39, 46 and 48.

[57] *ibid.*, p. 51.

preaching on the Resurrection, he roused them wonder-fully to joy in the Lord'.[58] We tend not to think of Thomas as a preacher, so the text is worth noting. Thomas was, of course, by temperament and vocation, far more retiring than Dominic. What gave him the greatest joy in life was, without question, contemplative study or the pursuit of wisdom, an occupation or a task which, he tells us himself, is 'by common consent the most delightful of all virtuous activities'.[59] Thomas says further that: 'those who devote themselves to the contemplation of truth are the happiest anyone can be in this life.'[60]

No wonder, then, that William of Tocco, the saint's first biographer, says that Thomas inspired joy in all those who saw him.[61] And Bartholomew, another early source, declares that everyone believed that God was with him 'for he *always had a joyous countenance, sweet and affable*'.[62] These two reports may well be reliable. And yet we know that Thomas, from a young age, possessed a rather taciturn temperament. So can we trust the reports, or do they represent simply the bland commonplaces of medieval hagiography? I am inclined to the view that they are reliable, and my judgement is based, in part, on the attitude Thomas expresses, in his writings, towards such

[58] *ibid.*, p. 48.

[59] St Thomas Aquinas, *Sententia libri ethicorum*, X, 10, 1177 a 22, (Rome 1969) p. 584.

[60] *ibid.*, X, 11, 1177 b 31, p. 588.

[61] See Jean-Pierre Torrell O.P., *St Thomas Aquinas: The Person and His Work* (Washington 1996) p. 280.

[62] Cited in Torrell, *St Thomas Aquinas*, p. 280.

things as charity, playfulness, friendship and good humour.

(a) Happiness and Good Humour

In the *Summa*, Thomas defends what he calls 'affability' and 'cheerfulness' - quite openly disagreeing with the view that austerity must always exclude 'cheerfulness' or must forbid 'the giving and receiving of the pleasures of conversation'.[63] What is more, Thomas takes to task those people who are so serious about themselves they never say anything laughable or funny (*nec ipsi dicunt aliquid ridiculum*), but instead are always trying to obstruct the fun or the amusement of others.[64] Such people are not only unpleasant company, according to Thomas, they are also morally unsound. He writes: 'Those who are lacking in fun, and who never say anything funny or humorous, but instead give grief to those who make jokes, not accepting even the modest fun of others, are morally unsound (*vitiosi*) and, in the view of the philosopher [Aristotle], are rough and boorish (*duri et agrestes*).'[65]

Of course, Thomas is well aware that even laughter and playfulness can, on occasion, be excessive and inappropriate. He would probably agree, for example, with Goethe's telling statement on the subject: 'Every century tries to make the sacred vulgar, the difficult easy, the serious hilarious - which really would not be objection-

---

[63] ST, II II, q.168, a.4, obj.3 and ad.3.
[64] ST, II II, q.168, a.4.
[65] *ibid.*

able at all if only earnestness and fun were not both
destroyed in the process.'[66] In spite of this danger,
however, Thomas, in the *Summa*, is prepared to openly
defend the playfulness and wit of professional actors and
comedians, remarking, for example, how 'it was revealed
to the Blessed Paphnutius that a certain jester (*ioculator*)
would be with him in the life to come'![67]

'Play,' in St Thomas' opinion, 'is necessary for the
intercourse of human life.'[68] He even states, at one point,
that an unrelenting seriousness indicates a lack of virtue
since 'it wholly despises play, which is as necessary for
human life as rest is'.[69] Nimbleness of wit, therefore, or
playfulness, can lay claim to be an authentic virtue.
Aristotle calls it *'eutrapelia'*. And the person who
possesses it, in Thomas' own words, 'has a happy turn
of mind, whereby he gives his words and deeds a cheerful
turn'.[70] In this spirit, Thomas - directly inspired by Cicero
- offers the following practical advice to public speakers:
'When the audience is weary, it will not be unhelpful to

[66] Cited by Josef Pieper in *Uber die Liebe*. See *Josef Pieper: An Anthology* (San Francisco 1984) p. 42.

[67] ST, II II, q.168, obj.3 and ad.3.

[68] ST, II II, q.168, a.3, ad.3.

[69] St Thomas Aquinas, *Sententia libri ethicorum*, IV, 16, 1128 b 2,
p. 258. Clearly at one with St Thomas' viewpoint on the subject of
play, the poet W.H. Auden remarks: 'among the half dozen or so
things for which a man of honour should be prepared, if necessary, to
die, the right to play, the right to frivolity, is not the least.' See Auden,
The Poet and the City, in *Twentieth Century Poetry: Critical Essays and
Documents*, G. Martin and P.N. Furbank (eds) (London 1975) p. 194.

[70] ST, II II, q.168, a.2.

begin with something novel or amusing provided that the dignity of the subject does not rule out joking.'[71]

With that suggestion in mind, I want to interrupt our reflections at this point, not indeed to offer something 'amusing' but rather to share what I hope might be a piece of 'novel' information. Although many people are familiar with the poetry of Gerard Manley Hopkins, very few are aware, I suspect, that one of his poems was dedicated to an Irish Dominican, the famous preacher, Fr Thomas Burke. The poem, which was composed in Latin, has Burke as its central subject, but it also includes an interesting reflection on Aquinas.

These two men, Hopkins and Burke, the Jesuit and the Dominican, the poet and the preacher, met only once in April 1877, when Burke visited the Jesuit house at St Bueno's in Wales. In his poem, Hopkins speaks of Burke as someone completely taken up with the tasks of preaching, study and spiritual direction. But then, by way of qualification, Hopkins says of Burke, 'the whole man is not engrossed in these matters, or, if you like, he is completely engrossed in them, but in such a way that he can be light-hearted amid serious affairs, for he mingles jests with his sacred duties, so that neither his voice nor his facial expression remains always the same.'[72] He mingles jests with his sacred duties: '*intermiscet enim cum sacris ludicra curis.*' Not only does this phrase and, indeed, the

[71] ST, II II, q.168, a.2, ad.1.

[72] *To the Reverend Father, Brother Thomas Burke, O.P. on his visit to St. Bueno's College*, in *The Poetical Works of Gerard Manley Hopkins*, (Oxford 1990) p. 370.

entire passage characterise Tom Burke, the Irishman, it also captures very well a certain lightness of touch in the Dominican style and spirit, an exuberance, or a playfulness, wholly approved of, it would seem, by the other Thomas.

But what evidence do we have, in fact, that Aquinas himself 'mingled jests with his sacred duties'? Is there evidence anywhere in his life of 'a happy turn of mind'? Remigio, one of Thomas' students in Paris, reports that Thomas once made a humorous allusion in class to the extravagant liturgical celebrations which had been held for the feast of St Martin, in contrast to more modest celebrations for the feast of St Peter.[73] The local people (*rustici*) had, it seems, attributed to Martin's intercession the amazingly abundant harvest of that year. But St Peter's contribution to the harvest was not noted. So, it would seem that, by the common consent of the faithful, St Peter's feast that year was, by comparison with St Martin's, somewhat down-graded!

Apart from this one story, have we any other evidence of Aquinas' sense of humour? The Dominican, Father Torrell, in his superb, two-volume work on Aquinas, notes that although 'we have no indication of the frequency of such sallies ... what we know from other sources about the vivacity of Thomas' reactions, inclines us to think that they were not rare'.[74] I agree with this suggestion. But I am inclined to think, nevertheless, that far more important than the existence of actual 'jokes'

[73] See Torrell, *St Thomas Aquinas*, p. 281.
[74] *ibid.*

told by Aquinas, is the presence in his work of what we might call a certain pervasive attitude. 'Humour,' as Ludwig Wittgenstein once shrewdly observed, 'is not a mood but a way of looking at the world.'[75] That being said, however, I hope it will not seem forced or wilful if I draw attention here to a passage from Aquinas which I have never seen quoted, but which I suspect would almost certainly have brought a smile to the lips of his students when they first read it.

The passage occurs in Thomas' commentary on the fourth book of Aristotle's *Ethics*. Thomas is reflecting at one point on beauty, and in particular on that beauty which can be found 'in a large body'. Now we all know – and from a number of sources – that Brother Thomas was not slim. '*Grossus et brunus*' are two of the adjectives used to describe him.[76] And Remigio of Florence, his student in Paris, does not hesitate to speak of his famous master as a very fat man indeed – '*pinguissimus*'![77] Thomas, in his commentary on the *Ethics*, is generous enough, echoing 'the philosopher', to suggest that 'those who are small might be called pretty (*formosi*) because of an appropriateness of colour and a fitting proportion of limbs'.

[75] Wittgenstein made this observation while staying at Rosro in Ireland. See Ray Monk, *Ludwig Wittgenstein: The Duty of Genius* (London 1991) p. 529.

[76] Nicolas de Piperno: Naples 19. Cited in Torrell, *St Thomas Aquinas*, p. 278.

[77] See Torrell, *St Thomas Aquinas*, p. 278.

However, he goes on at once to add: 'they cannot be called beautiful because of a lack of magnitude.'[78]

It is almost certain that Thomas never delivered this commentary on Aristotle in a public, university forum. But, according to V.J. Bourke, the commentary may have been shared in private by Thomas with some of his own brethren, 'quite possibly as a lecture course for young students in the Roman Province of the Order of Preachers'.[79] If he did so, one can have no difficulty imagining the students' reaction, when, standing four-square in front of them, Master Thomas – with conscious or unconscious irony – placidly declared: *'pulcritudo proprie consistit in corpore magno'*: 'beauty is found in a large body'![80]

(b) Wisdom and the Beatitudes

Within the Christian spiritual tradition, Thomas' reflections on good humour and playfulness have unfortunately received little attention. And the same is true, sad

[78] St Thomas Aquinas, *Sententia libri ethicorum*, IV, 8, 1123 b, 5 pp. 226-7.

[79] See V.J. Bourke, *The Nicomachean Ethics and Thomas Aquinas*, in *St Thomas Aquinas: Commemorative Studies*, A.A. Maurer (ed.) (Toronto 1974) p. 250. See also p. 248.

[80] St Thomas Aquinas, *Sententia*, IV, 8, 1123 b 5. G.K. Chesterton, in his book on Aquinas, writes: 'His bulk made it easy to regard him humorously ... It may be that he, and not some irritated partisan ... was responsible for the sublime exaggeration that a crescent was cut out of the dinner-table to allow him to sit down.' G.K. Chesterton, *St Thomas Aquinas* (London 1933) p. 97.

to say, concerning something far more important – Thomas' teaching in the *Summa* and elsewhere on happiness or '*beatitude*'. Many scholars are inclined to highlight Thomas' debt to Aristotle, and of course his debt to the Greek is enormous. But the deepest sources of Thomas' fascination with, and understanding of, happiness are not to be found buried away somewhere in Greek philosophy. They are to be found, first and last, in the manifest joy of Gospel truth, and in the witness to that joy and that truth given by Dominic and by the Friars Preachers.

The joy of Gospel truth – the full paradox of that joy – finds its most telling expression in the Beatitudes. And it is perhaps significant that in St Matthew's Gospel – St Dominic's favourite Gospel – the Beatitudes are deliberately placed at the beginning of the Sermon on the Mount. Together with the Sermon, they not only sum up, according to Aquinas, 'the whole process of forming the life of the Christian',[81] they constitute the text in the New Testament which most distinguishes the New Law as distinct from the Decalogue or the Old Law.

Sadly, however, for 400 years, Thomas' teaching on the New Law has been all but ignored by the great majority of moral theologians. With the rise of legalistic casuistry in the sixteenth century, a concept of morality was developed which focused almost exclusively on obligation. St Thomas, staying closer to the spirit of the Gospel, indicates that, in the Sermon on the Mount, as well as

[81]   ST, I II, q.108, a.3.

having our attention drawn to 'the various precepts of the law', we are also made aware that our lives in this world and in the next are ordered towards happiness.[82] In his book, *The Pursuit of Happiness*, the contemporary Dominican theologian, Servais Pinckaers, writes:

> Promises of happiness come first in God's Word and designs ... As St Paul understood so well, this ordering has enormous consequences for life and for the moral issues of revelation. Salvation, freedom, justice, and happiness come to us from our faith in the divine promises and our hope in mercy and grace, rather than from the merits we may acquire by our own strength in adhering to the observances of the law.[83]

St Thomas, like St Dominic before him, was deeply grounded in the teaching of St Paul and in the Gospel of Matthew. He understood that the Beatitudes and the Sermon on the Mount represent God's answer to our human search for happiness. 'We can literally say that the Gospel teaches a morality of beatitude or blessedness,' writes Servais Pinckaers. 'Obligations are not ruled out – we need them – but they are secondary and instrumental.'[84] Morality, then, is placed not so much under the rubric of obligation by St Thomas but rather under the rubric of happiness. In fact, it is worth noting that, in the entire *prima secundae* of the *Summa*, where Thomas

[82] ST, I II, q.108, a.3.
[83] Servais Pinckaers O.P., *The Pursuit of Happiness* (New York 1998) p. 27.
[84] ibid., p. viii.

discusses morality, there is not one single article devoted exclusively to obligation![85]

So Thomas, like the great Augustine, refuses to have the question of happiness set aside. For both men, morality begins with happiness, and is a search for happiness. 'There is no doubt about it,' Augustine says, 'we all want to be happy. Everyone will agree with me even before the words are out of my mouth ... so let us see if we can find the best way to achieve it.'[86] Unfortunately, very seldom if ever, in the manual theologies of later centuries, do we find such a frank and honest admission of our human thirst for happiness. But it is precisely this thirst which contemplatives like Aquinas and Augustine, Eckhart and Catherine, never for a moment allowed themselves to forget. These great preachers of the Gospel who, to their contemporaries, appeared so completely radiant, discovered, in their own search for happiness, something unexpected about its attainment. And it must have struck them with the surprise and force of a Gospel paradox. For 'the secret' they uncovered was, in a sense, not to pursue happiness at all, at least not for themselves alone. But, instead, by learning step by step to give their attention to God and to their neighbour, and by seeking, wherever possible, to bring fullness of life and joy to others, happiness - and very great happiness indeed - came to them in abundance.

[85] See Servais Pinckaers O.P., *The Sources of Christian Ethics* (Edinburgh 1995) p. 17.

Conclusion

Happiness – what Robert Louis Stevenson once described as the 'great task of happiness' – has been the theme of this chapter. Like a piece of string held onto, it has led us back to reflect on an aspect of the Dominican tradition, at once wholly delightful yet also profoundly challenging: happiness, first, as manifested in the lives of some early Dominicans; then, as expressed in certain texts from the Dominican mystical tradition; and, finally, as present in the life and work of a theologian of genius, Thomas Aquinas. As we have gone along on this journey, we have always found ourselves in the company of Dominican men and women, but in different times and in different places: in a contemplative convent at Bologna, for example, with Diana d'Andolò; in a classroom with St Thomas Aquinas at Paris; in the streets and squares of Italy with Jordan of Saxony and his band of preachers; and in Germany at Mass with Blessed Henry Suso. But from each one of these Dominicans we have been learning about joy, and in particular about Gospel joy. For the string held onto has led us, in the end, to the top of the Mountain of the Beatitudes. And there, in company with Dominic and Jordan, with Catherine and Diana, with Thomas, Eckhart and Suso, with Margaret and Mechtild, we have found ourselves listening, as before, but with a new understanding, perhaps, and with a deeper sense of poverty and wonder, to Christ's own words, his own remarkable teaching about human happiness.

---

[86] St Augustine, *De moribus eccclesiae catholicae*, I, iii, 4, PL, 32; p. 1312, cited in Pinckaers, *The Pursuit of Happiness*, p. vii.

3

'Eat the Book':
Study in the Dominican
Tradition

The place of study in the Dominican tradition is clearly indicated in the following short passage from Blessed Humbert of Romans. In his 'Treatise on the Formation of Preachers' he writes:

> Though a grace of preaching is strictly had by God's gift, a sensible preacher still ought to do what he can to ensure that his preaching is commendable, by carefully studying what he has to preach ... So Jerome says, in his comment on Ezekiel 3:1, 'Eat the book': 'The words of God should be stored up in our hearts and carefully examined, and only then proffered to the people.'[1]

---

[1] Humbert of Romans, *Treatise on the Formation of Preachers*, VII, 82, in S. Tugwell, *Early Dominicans: Selected Writings* (New York 1982), p. 205.

Two things are immediately clear from this passage. First, in the context of Dominican life and vocation, study is not undertaken for its own sake but for the purpose of preaching the Word of God. And, second the study envisaged, although it clearly presupposes some form of academic commitment, indicates something else as well. There is a quality of attention demanded that engages the whole person. Thus Humbert notes that the words of God are not only to be examined, they are to be *devoured*, and so not merely appropriated by our minds in an abstract, scientific manner with a mere superficial understanding, but somehow interiorized and absorbed or, as he puts it himself, 'stored up in our hearts'.

Humbert makes no mention of prayer in this passage, but there is, of course, an obvious link between the preacher's life of prayer and contemplation and what Humbert is insisting on here. But what is this link exactly? How did the Dominicans of the first few generations, for example, understand the relationship between dedicated commitment to study and the life of prayer? And why did they insist on making so unbreakable the link between such study and the call to be preachers of the Word?

Study as a Spiritual Work

In modern times, holiness has come to be associated with the heart rather than with the head. A dedication to study is sometimes perceived, in fact, as being a positive hindrance to the pursuit of holiness. And we are constantly being encouraged by contemporary authors to make a journey, an exodus, out from the captivity of the so-called dry and grey intellect, to the fresh and living springs of the heart. This dualism, however, between head and heart is something quite foreign to the Dominican spirit and understanding. Actual goodness, it is true, can certainly be considered as the holiness of the heart, since from there charity springs. But thinking, serious thinking about the Gospel, and about the world we are living in, can itself be a form of holiness – and a necessary form. Accordingly, Dominicans in every age tend to insist that there can be no serious awakening to God without an awakening in the mind. For, as disciples of the Word, we discover at the end if not at the beginning of our studies that, whereas goodness may indeed be the holiness of the heart, *truth is the holiness of the mind*.

When the holiness of Thomas Aquinas is referred to in *The Dialogue* of St Catherine of Siena, it is characterized by one striking phrase: Thomas saw God in his 'mind's eye' (*ne l'occhio de l'intelletto*).[2] Now St Thomas, we know from early sources, was a man capable, on occasion, of profound spiritual emotion. He had, for example, the gift of tears. But for Thomas, as for many of the early Dominicans, thinking itself was a sacred activity. His mind was a mind in love with God. Owing to the great intellectual genius of St Thomas and that of others in the Order before and after him, a devotion to learning came to be regarded as a distinctive characteristic of Dominicans. But how fundamental, in the very early years of the

---

[2] St Catherine of Siena, *Il Dialogo della divina providenza*, LXXXV, G. Cavallini (ed.) (Rome 1968) p. 192.

Order's development, was this concern for study? Can we say that such a passionate devotion to learning had been, from the beginning, a vital aspect of the Dominican spirit?

The Example of Dominic

The dedication of Dominic himself to a life of study is underlined in one of the first pages of Jordan of Saxony's important work, *On the Beginnings of the Order of Preachers*. Jordan writes: '[Dominic's] eagerness to imbibe the streams of holy scripture was so intense and so unremitting that he spent whole nights almost without sleep, so untiring was his desire to study.'[3] Moreover, since 'he accepted the Lord's commandments so warmly,' and since 'his love and piety fertilized whatever he learned,' Dominic, we are told, 'was able to penetrate the mysteries of difficult theological questions with the humble understanding of his heart'.[4] With Dominic, it would seem, the commitment to theological study was almost instinctive. As early as 1215 or 1216, he was seen attending, with a small number of his brothers, the theology lectures being given at Toulouse by the English theologian, Alexander Stavensby. And, within a few years, he had sent a number of his fledgling Dominicans to both Paris and Bologna, the centres of theological learning at

[3] Jordan of Saxony, *Libellus de principiis ordinis praedicatorum*, 7, in MOPH, XVI, p. 28; trans., S. Tugwell, *Jordan of Saxony: On the Beginnings of the Friars Preachers* (Dublin 1982), I, 7, p. 1.
[4] ibid., 7, pp. 28-9; *Jordan of Saxony: On the Beginnings of the Friars Preachers*, pp. 1-2.

that time. One of the witnesses at Dominic's canonization process, Brother John of Spain, remarked that he '*always* carried around with him the Gospel of Matthew and the letters of Paul', and 'studied them so much that he knew them by heart.'[5] That word 'always', with regard to study, is surely significant. John of Spain tells us further that he '*always* advised and exhorted his brothers to study both the Old and New Testaments'.[6]

In the early iconography of the saint, Dominic is most often shown holding a book in his hands. And this detail is by no means accidental. For the book, especially the book of the Gospels, was central to Dominic, both in his life of study and in his life of prayer. In the thirteenth-century text, *The Nine Ways of Prayer* [of St Dominic], we are informed that the preacher, 'sober and alert and anointed with a spirit of devotion ... would sit down to read or pray, recollecting himself in himself and fixing himself in the presence of God.'[7] Further, with a book open before him, '[w]hen he was reading like this on his own, he used to venerate the book and bow to it and sometimes kiss it, particularly if it was a book of the gospels or if he was reading the words which Christ had spoken with his own lips'.[8]

---

[5] *Acta canonizationis s. Dominici*, 29, in MOPH, XVI (Rome 1935) p. 147. Italics added.

[6] *ibid*. Italics added.

[7] Eighth Way of Prayer, *The Nine Ways of Prayer* [of St Dominic] in S. Tugwell, *Early Dominicans*, p. 101.

[8] *ibid*.

These statements about Dominic, with regard to prayer and study, recall that short, vivid imperative, 'Eat the book,' which Humbert of Romans quoted from chapter three of Ezekiel. In the Ezekiel passage, after the words 'eat the book' or 'eat the scroll', the text continues: 'I opened my mouth; he gave me the scroll to eat and said, "Son of man, feed and be satisfied by the scroll I am giving you." I ate it, and it tasted sweet as honey' (Ezek. 3:2-3). Like the prophet Ezekiel, St Dominic, it can be said, devoured with enthusiasm the scroll or book of God's word. First he read it and then he tasted it. It should come as no surprise, therefore, to find Jordan of Saxony alluding to a similar text from the Old Testament when, in the *Libellus*, he speaks of Dominic's hunger and thirst for truth. Jordan writes: 'He began to develop a passionate appetite for God's words, finding them "sweeter than honey to his mouth."'[9] But, for Dominic, it was not so much the experience of the Word or the taste of the Word that mattered most, but rather the Word itself, and the mission he received to *speak* the Word. Of supreme importance, therefore, is the following brief sentence in the Ezekiel text: 'Son of man, eat what is given to you; eat this scroll, then *go and speak to the house of Israel*' (Ezek. 3:1).[10] Dominic, we can be sure, would not have overlooked that final injunction. He was to be a preacher, first and last.

[9] *Libellus*, 6, p. 28; *Jordan of Saxony: On the Beginnings of the Friars Preachers*, p. 1. (See Psalm 119:103: 'How sweet are thy words to my taste, sweeter than honey to my mouth!')
[10] Italics added.

Study into Preaching

In the Prologue to the early Dominican *Constitutions*, a text which of course St Dominic himself would have overseen, study is not only mentioned but given an unusual weight and importance. Clearly, for the early friars, a man who is a Dominican is a man committed to study. But the fact that, in these early Constitutions, study commands such unusual attention, is due to one overriding factor, and that is, of course, the service which study can give to the task of 'preaching and the salvation of souls'. '[A]ll our concern (*studium nostrum*),' we read in the Prologue, 'should be primarily and passionately directed to this all-important goal.'[11] That statement is fundamental. So absorbing in itself can study become at times that, far from serving the work of the apostolate, it can begin actually to undermine the focus on preaching. However, in spite of this risk, Dominicans over the centuries have followed Dominic's lead in emphasizing the importance of study in the preacher's life. Thus, for example, in a long commentary on the Constitutions by Blessed Humbert of Romans, *Expositio super Constitutiones*, we read: 'Study is not the end of the Order, but it is an utmost necessity to that end, which is preaching and labouring for the salvation of souls, for without study we can do neither.'[12]

[11] Prologue, *The Early Dominican Constitutions*, in S. Tugwell, *Early Dominicans*, p. 457.

[12] Humbert of Romans, *Expositio super Constitutiones*, XII, in *Opera de vita regulari*, II, J.J. Berthier (ed.) (Rome 1889) p. 41. Note also, in the *Expositio*, the section entitled *De utilitate studii in nostro ordine*, VIII, pp. 28-31. Although every Dominican was expected to study, not

Dominic, in his attempts to refute the errors of the Cathar heretics in Provence, had made this discovery for himself. He came to realize that, in terms of apostolic strategy, it would not be wise simply to deliver moral exhortations to the people, and ignore the challenge to orthodoxy. What was needed, if the truth of God's Word was to be defended, and the Christian vision upheld, was an accurate and profound knowledge of scripture and of church teaching. And the only way to acquire such knowledge was through rigorous study. This realization, on the part of Dominic, was to have enormous consequences for the formation of his new Order. According to *The Dialogue* of St Catherine of Siena, in marked contrast to Francis of Assisi, whose hallmark was poverty, the hallmark of Dominic (though himself a poor mendicant) was 'learning' (*la scientia*).[13] In *The Dialogue*, the Father explains to Catherine that it was precisely 'in order to stamp out the errors that were rising up at that time' that Dominic built the foundation of his Order on 'the light of learning'.[14]

Cont.

every Dominican was expected to be a great scholar. Once, when Jordan of Saxony was fiercely attacked by the brethren for having encouraged into the Order young men who were not particularly intelligent or educated, Jordan replied: 'Let them be ... I tell you that you will see many of them ... turn out to be splendid preachers, through whom the Lord will work more for the salvation of souls than he does through many more intelligent and educated men.' See Thomas of Cantimpré, *Bonum universale de apibus*, II, xix, 2 (Douai 1627) p. 227; translation in S. Tugwell, *Early Dominicans*, p. 132.

[13] *Il Dialogo*, 158, p. 463.
[14] *ibid.*, 158, pp. 459-60.

Study and Formation

Study was considered so important in Dominican formation that, in the earliest legislation of the Order, local superiors were given authority to dispense the brethren from anything that might interrupt their studies.[15] Even the novices, though naturally encouraged to give time to prayer, were also expected to be 'earnest ... in their study, always reading or thinking about something by day or by night ... striving to retain as much as they can in their minds'.[16] That distinctly Dominican suggestion – to be always 'thinking about something' – finds an echo, centuries later, in the advice the famous preacher Vincent McNabb gave to the young Dominicans of the English Province. 'Think of anything,' he would say to them, 'but for God's sake think!'[17]

The kind of commitment to study which St Dominic demanded of his young Friars Preachers may not, perhaps, strike us today as being all that surprising. But, again and again in the history of religion, there has been an unfortunate tendency on the part of committed religious people to suspect intellectual endeavour, as if the awakening of the mind were in itself somehow subversive of the life of piety. Thus, even the great St

[15] Prologue, *The Early Dominican Constitutions*, in S. Tugwell, *Early Dominicans*, p. 457.

[16] *The Early Dominican Constitutions*, 13, in S. Tugwell, *Early Dominicans*, p. 466.

[17] Cited in 'Anniversary Sermon for Fr Vincent McNabb' by Hilary J. Carpenter, O.P., in *A Vincent McNabb Anthology: Selections from the Writings of Vincent McNabb O.P.*, F.E. Nugent (ed.) (London 1955) p. ix.

Teresa of Avila, a woman normally respectful of the need, in her own spiritual life, for learned advice and informed knowledge of the faith, could declare: 'The less I understand the more I believe; and this brings me greater devotion.'[18]

Such a sharp dialectic between learning and devotion has found expression, over the centuries, in innumerable pious texts concerning the spiritual life. In one such text, for example, *The Imitation of Christ*, the pride and power of the intellect comes under relentless attack and, in one short vivid aphorism, the scientific impulse is, for a moment, peremptorily dismissed: 'I would rather feel compunction than know its definition.'[19] Centuries earlier, a statement concerning devotion and study was made in an encyclical letter to the Dominican Order by Blessed Jordan of Saxony. For Jordan, a considerable problem in the formation of the younger brethren was not that they gave too much attention to study but too little. They simply did not commit themselves enough, he felt, to their academic tasks. 'In some cases,' Jordan says, 'this is because they do not want to be distracted from their *unintelligent devotions*.'[20]

---

[18] *Relaciones espirituales XXXIII*, in *Obras de Santa Teresa de Jesus*, Silverio de Santa Teresa O.C.D. (ed.) (Burgos 1915) p. 63.

[19] Thomas à Kempis, *The Imitation of Christ*, trans., R. Challoner (Dublin 1915) p. 3. Elsewhere in *The Imitation* we read: 'Leave off that excessive desire of knowing, because there is found therein much distraction and deceit' pp. 5-6.

[20] Jordan of Saxony, *Encyclical Letter, May 1233*, in S. Tugwell, *Early Dominicans*, p. 123. Italics added.

Now Jordan does not intend here, for an instant, to undermine the spirit of devotion in the younger friars. But, being himself a servant of the Word and an active preacher of the Gospel, he is worried, it would seem, that these young Dominicans might fail to grasp the Gospel vision, and focus exclusively on their own private pieties and devotions. If they do that, Jordan warns, the results will be grave. Apart from 'neglecting their own benefit,' they will, he says, 'deprive many people of a chance of salvation, when they could have helped them on their way to eternal life if only they had studied properly'.[21]

Preachers of Learning and Zeal

In the twelth canto of the *Paradiso*, when Dante begins to speak of St Dominic and of his passion to proclaim the word of truth, he speaks of him not only as an educated man and preacher of the gospel but almost as a force of nature: 'Then with both learning and zeal (*con dottrina e con volere*) and with the apostolic office, he went forth like a torrent driven from a high spring.'[22] Dominic's own contemporaries were themselves well aware of the

---

[21] *ibid.*, pp. 123-4. In the *Vitae Fratrum* the story is told of a pious German friar who experienced so much pleasure in contemplation that 'he put aside all study'. However, 'his brethren, noting his conduct, accused him of making himself unfit for the duties of the Order by not applying himself to study.' *De progressu ordinis*, IV, 5, ii, in *Vitae Fratrum*, MOPH, I, B.M. Reichert, O.P. (ed.) (Louvain 1896) pp. 160-1.

[22] *Il Paradiso*, Canto XII, 97-99, in *The Divine Comedy: Paradiso* (Oxford 1971) p. 179.

preacher's utter dedication to his task. One witness at the canonization process remarked that Dominic was 'so enthusiastic as a preacher that by day and by night, in churches, houses, fields, on the road, everywhere, he wanted to preach the word of the Lord and he encouraged the brethren to do the same and not to talk about anything except God.'[23] His compassion extended, we are told, 'not only to the faithful, but also to pagans and unbelievers and even the damned in hell, and he wept a great deal for them.'[24]

Dominic, it is clear, possessed a strong instinct for adventure. He was daring both by nature and by grace. Dante calls him '*il santo atleta*', the holy athlete.[25] No matter how difficult or unforeseen the challenge of the hour, he was not afraid to take enormous risks for the sake of the Gospel. It is hardly surprising, therefore, that within a few years it could be said of the young friars who followed in his wake, and whom he himself had dispersed far and wide to preach the gospel, that they had made the ocean their cloister.[26] But was this spirit of

[23] The witness, Abbot William Pierre, gave his testimony at the Languedoc canonization process. See *Acta canonizationis s. Dominici*, 18, pp. 182-3. The translation is by S. Tugwell in *Dominic* by Vladimir Koudelka, O.P. (London 1997) p. 138.

[24] This testimony was given at the Bologna canonization process by Brother Ventura. See *Acta canonizationis s. Dominici*, 11, p. 132. See Koudelka, 104, p. 122.

[25] *Il Paradiso*, Canto XII, 56; *The Divine Comedy: Paradiso*, p. 176.

[26] That splendid observation came from the pen of Matthew Paris in the middle of the thirteenth century. It was not intended, however, as a compliment. Paris contrasted the 'decent and orderly' life of

risk and adventure reflected in the *intellectual* life of the first Dominicans? Study, we know, was given a place that was unheard of before in the history of religious life. It was no longer simply one exercise among others. It was now a central and sacred task. But, in terms of actual content and imaginative range, how striking and original were the studies of these first friars? The principal point to be made, in answer to this question, is that the early Dominicans were not attempting to be 'striking and original'. Their studies were shaped by the needs of others, and given the nature of the crisis at that time, what was most urgently required for the task of preaching and the *cura animarum* was straightforward moral and doctrinal cathechesis. Dominicans were, of course, subsequently to be at the forefront of 'the new learning' in most of the great universities of Europe. But that was a development which came slowly, and far more so, perhaps, than most scholars realized until recently.

In a comprehensive and helpful study on the shape of Dominican studies before 1350, M. Michèle Mulchahey has drawn our attention to what she calls 'the essential conservatism of early Dominican education'.[27] Since the

---

Cont.
enclosed religious with the outrageous freedom of the friars who, instead of remaining all the time in their monasteries, were out 'wandering round the towns and countryside'. See *Chron. maiora* V (Rolls Series 57e) p. 529; cited in S. Tugwell, *The Way of the Preacher* (London 1981) p. 13.

[27] M. Michèle Mulchahey, '*First the Bow is Bent in Study': Dominican Education before 1350* (Toronto 1998) p. 54.

Order was founded to combat heresy, its first educational goal, Mulchahey notes, was to ensure the orthodoxy of its own members. Accordingly, the range of educational focus did not stretch very wide for quite a number of years. The immediate task, and the most important, was to gain knowledge of scripture and right doctrine. There was no encouragement, therefore, to read widely in 'the books of the pagans and philosophers'. In fact, by a special clause inserted in the *Constitutions* of 1220, the preachers were instructed to read 'only theological books'.[28] Gradually, of course, the shape of Dominican education began to change. In a sense, parallel to Dominic's own original desire to go to the furthest frontiers of human need, and his manifest willingness to hold dialogue with all kinds of people, the Friars Preachers found themselves able, in time, to devote sustained and serious attention both to the secular sciences and to the writings of 'the pagans and philosophers'. One of the great pioneers in this regard, if not the greatest, was Albertus Magnus.

A Revolutionary Intellectualism

In the second half of the thirteenth century, a small number of Dominicans, directly inspired by the example

---

[28] 'Primitive Constitutions,' XXVIII, in *Saint Dominic: Biographical Documents,* F.C. Lehner, O.P. (ed.) (Washington 1964) p. 245. The admonition concerning pagan or secular writings was not something peculiar to the Friars Preachers. It represented, in fact, one of the ordinary norms or rules for clerical education at that time. See Mulchahey, *Dominican Education*, p. 57.

of Albert as a thinker, and by his dogged insistence on the importance of philosophy and the sciences, began to move to the frontiers of human thought and scholarship. M-D. Chenu, in a paper entitled 'The Revolutionary Intellectualism of St Albert', writes:

> At a certain point medieval Christianity found itself at the cross-roads, it encountered science. That was a grave moment; should the Christian, in order to assure himself of heavenly things, keep himself apart from earthly ones? Many did not know what to make of that 'science' which presented itself already fully equipped, rich with the treasures of antiquity, handed on and enlarged by Arab civilization ... To the question whether science should be received many replied: No. Albert answered: Yes.[29]

But was Albert's response to the challenge of science in his time all that remarkable? Chenu argues that it marked nothing less than a revolution in human and philosophical thought. He contrasts Albert's 'daring prevision' and wholly positive response to the science of his time with the 'misguided refusal' on the part of later thinkers and theologians when faced with the challenge of science in their own day.[30] What is more, Chenu refuses to make the scientific renaissance of the thirteenth century a kind of

[29] M-D. Chenu, O.P., 'The Revolutionary Intellectualism of St. Albert', *Blackfriars* 19 (1938) pp. 5–15. For a more recent and more detailed assessment of Albert's contribution to the development of science, see William A. Wallace, *The Scientific Methodology of St Albert the Great*, in *Albertus Magnus Doctor Universalis 1280/1980*, G. Meyer and A. Zimmermann (eds) (Mainz 1980) pp. 385–407.

[30] *ibid.*, p. 6.

poor cousin to that of the fifteenth. Both periods, in his opinion, are distinguished by a kind of 'intellectual inebriation'. In fifteenth-century Florence, for example, 'the literary and artistic intoxication' took the form of 'a very epidemic of learning, a delight of the mind in the joy of thinking, the supreme gladness of an intellectual feast'.[31] But the ferment of ideas in the Paris of St Albert was no less remarkable. Reflecting on that period, Chenu does not hesitate to declare: 'the intellectual inebriation of the Paris of 1250 was deeper, let us even say more revolutionary. It was not a revelation of plastic beauty in the realm of imagination and sensibility; it was a revelation of nature, of its truth, its being, in the realm of intelligence.'[32]

Almost, we can say, like a first Adam on the earth, in the middle of the thirteenth century Albert of Cologne began to look at the world around him with a completely fresh gaze. In his commentary on Matthew's Gospel he wrote: 'The whole world is theology for us, because the heavens proclaim the glory of God.'[33]

---

[31] *ibid.*, p. 11.

[32] *ibid.*, p. 74. Chenu refers loosely here to the Paris of 1250, but Albert had almost certainly left Paris for Cologne two years earlier.

[33] *In Evangelicum secundum Matthaeum*, 13:35, in *Opera omnia B. Alberti Magni*, vol. XX, A. Borgnet (ed.) (Paris 1893) p. 571; cited in *Albert and Thomas: Selected Writings*, S. Tugwell O.P. (ed.) (New York 1988) p. 29.

The Example of Albert the Great

Albert was a man, a scholar, possessed like no other in his generation by a curiosity – almost a compulsion – to understand and annotate the multiple wonders of creation. Nothing, it seemed, in the living world, nothing in the air above his head, nothing that moved on the earth itself, or in the rivers, or in the vast oceans, escaped his notice. He wrote treatises on astronomy, chemistry, grammar, botany, zoology, biology, logic and mathematics. In his treatise, *De caelo et mundo,* when considering the size and shape of the earth, he employed not only basic visual observation but also 'mathematical methods' (*signa sumpta ex Mathematicis*) in order to confirm that the world is round.[34]

At all times the sharpness of his perception is manifest, whether his attention is turned to the greatest or to the smallest things in creation. Thus, for example, in *De animalibus,* when discussing the eating habits of the eel, he dismisses outright Aristotle's idea that the creature feeds exclusively on slime. Albert writes: 'I have seen how it eats frogs, worms, and bits of fish, and how, with bait such as these, it is caught with a rod.'[35] Albert was fascinated by the tackle and trade of every profession. He tells us, for example, that he studied closely 'how they worked in copper in Paris and Cologne and other places

---

[34] *De caelo et mundo*, 2, IV, xi, in *ibid*, vol. IV (Paris 1890) p. 232.

[35] *De animalibus*, 7, I, iii, in *ibid.*, vol. XI (Paris 1891) pp. 372-3; cited in Hieronymus Wilms, O.P., *Albert the Great: Saint and Doctor of the Church* (London 1933) p. 32.

EAT THE BOOK':

where I have lived.'[36] Given such an extraordinary
passion to seek out the truth of things, it is no surprise
to learn that Albert was as great a teacher as he was a
scholar, and a notable preacher as well. For, far from
being a taciturn, solitary ascetic climbing up the mountain
of truth *alone to the Alone*, his constant joy as a teacher, he
tells us himself, was to search for the truth together with
his companions.[37]

The newness or freshness of the Dominican approach
to religious life and to study is brought clearly into focus
if we compare the sheer delight enjoyed by Albert and
others in the task of preaching and teaching with the grim
formula of St Jerome regarding the conduct of religious.
'The duty of the monk,' St Jerome declares, 'is to weep not
to teach.'[38] That centuries-old image of the religious man
or monk was an image or a mirage which, for several
years, seemed to haunt the margins of the lives of the
early Dominicans. We hear, for example, in the *Vitae
Fratrum*, of how the devil, 'the arch-deceiver', assumed on
occasion the disguise of an austere, monk-like figure in
order to make the first Dominicans feel guilty about a

[36] *De mineralibus*, 4, I, vi, in *Opera omnia B. Alberti*, vol. V (Paris
1890) p. 90.
[37] *Politica*, 8, vi, in *ibid.*, vol. VIII (Paris 1891) p. 804. See Yves
Congar, '*In dulcedine societatis quaerere veritatem*': Notes sur le travail en
équipe chez S. Albert et chez les prêcheurs au XIII siècle in Meyer, *Albertus
Magnus Doctor Universalis*, pp. 47-57.
[38] St Jerome, *Liber contra Vigilantium*, PL, XXIII, 351B. See
Reginald Ladner O.P., *The Plight of Preaching in the Twelfth Century*,
in Pierre Mandonnet O.P., *St. Dominic and His Work* (London 1944)
pp. 131-2. See also S. Tugwell, *Early Dominicans*, pp. 7-8.

95

number of the new dispensations which had been introduced into the Order for the sake of study and preaching. Not surprisingly, given the great success of his own preaching apostolate, Jordan of Saxony was one of the first to be visited in this way. The devil, we are told, in an exaggeratedly reverend disguise, appeared before him, and was heard at one point muttering to himself 'like a monk saying the psalter and the hours' (*quasi homo religious diceret psalmos et horas*).[39] Jordan, the preacher, was warned by the 'monk' that if he continued to dispense himself from the Rule he would be giving public scandal, and judgments, murmurs and disquiet would be the consequence. Fortunately, within days, Jordan was made to understand by God that the grave personage who had visited him, the rigid stickler for the law, was none other, in fact, than the devil himself, who had come to undermine the preacher 'from envy of the life he was living and envy of his preaching'.[40]

A similar kind of occurrence took place, we are told, in the life of Albert the Great. According to the report of Thomas of Cantimpré, when St Albert was at Paris he was visited by the devil disguised in the garb of a religious (*in specie cuiusdam fratris*).[41] The object of the devil's spleen, on this occasion, was St Albert's great devotion to the intellectual life. The text states explicitly that the evil one had come in order to draw the preacher away from study

---

[39] *Vitae Fratrum*, III, 28, p. 123, n.12.

[40] *ibid.*, p. 123.

[41] Thomas of Cantimpré, *Bonum universale de apibus*, II, lvii, 34, p. 563.

(*ut eum a studio revocaret*).[42] But Albert was alert to the devil's deceit. The idea that he, a son of Dominic and a preacher, should abandon study was immediately recognized as a gross temptation. Albert made the sign of the cross, and at once the apparition disappeared.[43]

Proud Scholars or Learned Apostles?

At the beginning of the second half of the thirteenth century, the Dominicans who were devoted to learning, such as St Albert the Great, and in general all the learned friars of the new mendicant orders, came under fierce attack. The man who led the charge was William of St Amour, a master at the University of Paris. His treatise, *De periculis novissimorum temporum* ('The Perils of the Last Times') took its title from St Paul's words to Timothy: 'Know this, that in the last days, will come dangerous times: men will be lovers of themselves, covetous, haughty, proud ... having indeed an appearance of piety but negating or denying the strength of piety' (2 Tim 3:1-5).[44] William of St Amour, in his attack on the new

---

[42] *ibid.*

[43] A play, based on the life of St Albert the Great, was published over 70 years ago by a Dominican of the Saulchoir. Of particular interest is the scene in which the devil tempts Albert to abandon study. See Claude Just (A-M Roguet O.P.), *Saint Albert le Grand célébré par personnages*, 2, IX (Paris 1932) pp. 61-5.

[44] The phrase 'an appearance of piety' does not occur in modern English translations of Paul's letter. But the Latin phrase *speciem pietatis* occurs in the Vulgate version of the letter with which, of course, Willliam of St Amour would have been familiar.

religious, pilloried the friars as men who were, in St Paul's words, 'always learning but never attaining to knowledge of the truth' (2 Tim. 3:7).[45] They were dangerous forerunners of the Antichrist, in his opinion, men dressed in a religious garb but devoted to study, and somehow able to wander at will all over the place, preaching in a distinctly learned manner, apostles radiant with the false light of secular learning.[46]

Among the new band of scholarly preachers under attack, the one who, in the end, decided to stand up to the challenge thrown down by William was St Albert the Great's most famous and most remarkable pupil, Friar Thomas d'Aquino. Answering point by point the arguments of William and others like him, Thomas demonstrated with clarity and simplicity that it is entirely suitable and necessary for religious, and especially for preachers, to be learned.[47] William had argued that, since religious were bound in a particular way to humility, they ought to refrain from acquiring knowledge altogether: 'Knowledge,' he declared, quoting St Paul, 'puffs up, but love builds up' (1 Cor 8:1). In his reply to this objection, Thomas acknowledged that knowledge or science could certainly lead to pride if it were not accompanied by

---

[45] All the details in this paragraph concerning the attack by William of St Amour on the friars are taken from the summary of that attack given by Aquinas in *Contra impugnantes Dei cultum et religionem*, chs. X–XI, in *Opera omnia s. Thomae Aquinatis*, vol. XLI (Rome 1970) pp. A130-A137.

[46] *ibid.*, ch. X, 1, pp. A130, and ch. XI, 1-2, pp. A131-A132.

[47] *ibid.*, ch. XI, 3, p. A133.

charity. But if those who were devoted to study were also devoted to works of charity, 'there would be little danger in learning'.[48] Then Thomas added, and with considerable verve: 'If we are to avoid knowledge because it leads to pride, we ought, on the same grounds, to desist from any good work.' [49]

It was, perhaps, to be expected that the learning of the Friars Preachers would, sooner or later, provoke opposition from outside the Order. But even within the ranks of the brethren themselves the new emphasis on learning met with some fierce opposition. Albert speaks, in one place, of people - some of them Dominicans - who, without any understanding of the subject, raise objections to the use of philosophy in the work of scholars and theologians like himself. And he notes that, even within the Order of Preachers, such people are not challenged. 'They are like brute animals,' he says, 'calling down anathemas on things of which they have not the slightest idea.'[50] In another place, Albert's exasperation with the enemies of study is even more manifest. Disturbed by the

[48] *ibid.*, XI, 4, 190–91, p. A134.

[49] *ibid.*, p. 79. Earlier, in the same text, Thomas gives short shrift to William's suggestion that the teaching of the friars was in direct contradiction with the 'perfect humility' of life to which they had vowed themselves. 'The notion,' he writes, 'that religious profess perfect humility is false. Religious make no vow of humility. Their vow is of obedience.' *ibid.*, II, 4, 530–33, p. A61. (I am grateful to my confrère, Charles Morerod O.P., for drawing my attention to this brief and robust rejoinder from Aquinas.)

[50] Albert the Great, *In Epistolam VII Dionysii*, 2, in *Opera omnia B. Alberti*, vol. XIV (Paris 1892) p. 910a.

way a few sour and lazy people were able to interfere with
the honest research undertaken by others, he writes:

> I make these remarks on account of certain idlers who,
> searching for a way to excuse or comfort their own idleness,
> confine their studies [literally their 'writings'] to fault-finding.
> And since they themselves are utterly lazy and sluggish
> (*torpentes in inertia*), in order not to be seen as lazy, they set
> about trying to spot blemishes in the great. These were the
> sort of people who killed Socrates, drove Plato from Athens
> and, through their machinations, conspired even to have
> Aristotle cast out.[51]

A considerable part of the opposition to learning
sprang, we may presume, from either jealousy or
ignorance. But there was also perhaps a more worthy
motive behind at least some of the doubts raised
concerning study. The principal point at issue was this,
and it is a question of no small importance for Dominican
spirituality: how will a radical commitment to study, on
the part of the preacher, affect his sense of devotion and
piety? Will it help or will it hinder the 'holy preaching'?

No one was more committed to research and study
than St Albert the Great. But he was not naive. He knew
that, like any other great gift in life, the gift of learning
could be taken up and used in the wrong way or in the
wrong spirit. And should that happen in the case of the
Friars Preachers, instead of dedicated study being a
wonderful aid to them in their preaching, it would

---

[51] Albert the Great, *Politica* in *Opera omnia B. Alberti*, vol. VIII,
pp. 803–4.

become a liability. It is no surprise, therefore, to find Albert the Great praying on one occasion: 'Lord Jesus Christ, graciously hear the voice of our sorrow ... that we may not be seduced by deceitful speech ... tempting us to the curiosity of knowledge (*curiositate scientiae*).'[52] For Albert there was nothing wrong with the impulse to explore the mystery of things, for that impulse was part of what one might call a kind of sacred curiosity, something wholly commendable. But there is another kind of curiosity or intellectual inquisitiveness which militates against the work of the preacher and even against the task of study itself. Accordingly, St Thomas, in spite of his own great passion for study and research, does not hesitate to point out that an inordinate curiosity, since it draws the mind away to superficial distractions, is a danger or a problem, and not only for study itself but for all other mental tasks and occupations.[53]

It was, we may presume, in part because of this danger that the early Dominicans took the trouble to note down a few stories about the early brethren which underlined the need, in the life of the preacher, for something more than a

[52] '*Oratio, IV*' (*Dominica quarta in adventu Domini*), *Orationes super evangelia dominicalia,* in *Opera omnia B. Alberti,* vol. XIII (Paris 1891) p. 346.

[53] See St Thomas Aquinas, *Contra impugnantes,* IX, 4, 6, p. A134. For a helpful reflection on *curiositas* in St Thomas, see Liam G. Walsh O.P., *St. Thomas and Study,* in *La Formazione integrale domenicana,* Robert Christian O.P. (ed.) (Bologna 1996) pp. 228ff. An earlier version of this paper was published in *The Renewal Papers* (Tallaght 1994) pp. 58-89.

commitment to study. One of the most vivid stories, for example, in the *Vitae Fratrum* concerns a certain friar who had a great fondness for philosophy. One day, finding himself in a state of rapture, he heard - coming, he believed, from the judgment seat of heaven - words of reproof and accusation: 'You are not a religious but a philosopher!'[54] The story repeats, as it happens, in almost all its details, an experience endured by St Jerome, centuries earlier, so it may or may not be true. But it does indicate a certain spiritual tension or concern in the minds and hearts of the early Dominicans with regard to learning. A century later, in *The Dialogue* of St Catherine of Siena, we read of preachers who are so absorbed in their research, and so inordinantly proud of their knowledge, they have become blind guides. They read scripture, the Father explains, but without understanding: 'They taste only its letter in their chasing after a multiplicity of books, never tasting the marrow of scripture.'[55] In the opinion of *The Dialogue,* these men, in thrall to a false curiosity, have lost the fundamental grace of the preacher, namely the 'hunger and longing for others' salvation'.[56]

Knowledge and Devotion

From the early days of the Order, the dangers attendant on a commitment to study were so clear, there was always a

[54] *Vitae Fratrum*, IV, 19, iii, pp. 208-9.
[55] *Il Dialogo*, 85, p. 194; translation in S. Noffke O.P., *Catherine of Siena: The Dialogue*, 85 (New York 1980) p. 157.
[56] *ibid.*, p. 81.

risk the Order might lose confidence in the identity given to it by Dominic, and focus exclusively on the life of prayer and devotion, ignoring the fact that the Order was founded, as *The Dialogue* puts it, 'on the light of learning' for the salvation of souls.[57] St Thomas Aquinas was well aware of Dominic's legacy, and in the *Summa* he confronts head on the question regarding radical commitment to learning and the life of devotion. To begin with, Thomas is honest about the risks, from a spiritual point of view, of becoming a learned individual. He writes: 'In knowledge and in every other endowment which belongs to greatness, man finds occasion to trust in himself rather than give himself over completely to God. And so, in the case of those who are gifted or learned, it can happen that these things are the occasion of devotion being hindered.'[58] In parenthesis here, it is interesting to note how Thomas' words concerning knowledge (*scientia*) are in some way prophetic of that extreme pride which can sometimes accompany our modern information technology, and prophetic also of the way science in particular has, over the centuries, tended to become detached from, and even disdainful of, the life of devotion. With regard, therefore, to the way Aquinas speaks about knowledge or '*scientia*', we might almost say what George Steiner said in another context concerning another author: '[he] seems to "hear" inside a word or a phrase the history of its future echoes.'[59]

[57] *ibid.*, 158, p. 459; *The Dialogue*, p. 337.

[58] ST, II II, q.82, a.3, ad.3.

[59] Cited in Alan Ecclestone, *A Staircase for Silence* (London 1977) p. 105.

In the *Summa* the sharp warning St Thomas gives us concerning the potential danger of learning does not constitute his most telling or his final pronouncement on the matter. That comes a few lines later when, in one short but crucial sentence, he says that, in spite of the obvious risks involved, 'if a man perfectly submits his learning and his other powers to God, his devotion, as a direct result, will be deepened.'[60] There, in that last phrase, Thomas strikes the characteristic Dominican note. The God to whom we are asked to surrender is the God of creation, so there can be no opposition between a commitment to science or learning and a life of devotion. On the contrary, even as devotion to God deepens, human knowledge or science, while always retaining its inherent, God-given freedom, begins to develop into wisdom. And, when that occurs, study is itself, we can say, a spirituality. 'The learned person,' Thomas writes in his commentary on *The Divine Names*, 'not only attains to knowledge of divine things, he also experiences them, i.e. not only does he receive them as knowledge into his mind, he also becomes one thing with them by love and by affection' (*non solum divinorum scientiam in intellectu accipiens, sed etiam diligendo, eis unitus est per affectum*).[61] Study, therefore, when deepened in this way, leads both to an increase of devotion in the student or theologian, and to actual communion with the divine.

[60] ST, II II, q.82, a.3, ad.3.
[61] See *Expositio in librum b. Dionysii de divinis nominibus*, no.191, Marietti (ed.) (Rome 1950) p. 59.

As much as anyone in the Christian tradition, St Thomas had great confidence in the power of the human intellect. But it is Thomas, the Angelic Doctor, who declares in the *Summa*: 'Neither a Catholic nor a pagan knows the nature of God as he is in himself.'[62] For St Thomas, even intimate communion with God does not imply that one somehow comprehends the entire mystery. Far from it. Thomas, according to Timothy Radcliffe, 'remained forever a man of questions, asking, searching, never satisfied, eager to learn from anyone'.[63] And Radcliffe continues: 'His central question which is a challenge for our day too, is the question: "What is God?" And his intellectual poverty and sanctity accepted defeat by this question. His respect for God's mystery ... implied his refusal of false images of God. It was the source of a permanent conversion to God's Word.'[64]

[62] ST, I, q.13, a.10, ad.5. In similar vein, St Thomas, commenting on Boethius' treatise, *On the Trinity*, writes: 'At the end of our knowledge, God is ultimately known as unknown, because then the mind knows God most perfectly when it knows that his essence is above all that can be known in this life of wayfaring.' In *Super Boetium de Trinitate* I, 2, ad. 1, in *Opera omnia* vol. L, p. 83.

[63] Timothy Radcliffe O.P., 'Letter to the Rector of the University of St Thomas, Manila, 20 January 1997', *Acta Magistri Ordinis,* ASOP, 105, fasc.I (January-April 1997) p. 33.

[64] *ibid.* This theme of knowing God by unknowing was taken up by other Dominicans after St Thomas, most notably by Meister Eckhart. Richard Woods O.P. gives particular attention to this important aspect of Dominican spirituality in *Mysticism and Prophecy: The Dominican Tradition* (London 1998). See also Paul Murray O.P., '[Meister Eckhart]: The Way of the Void', in *New Blackfriars*, 74, 869 (1993) 116-30.

Aquinas – as is well known – almost never speaks of himself in the first person. But there are one or two texts in which he comes near to doing precisely that, and the voice we hear is that of a genuinely humble man, a philosopher and theologian well aware of his great gifts, but even more aware of the enormity of the task he has undertaken. In the following passage, for example, from the opening pages of the *Summa contra Gentiles*, we are afforded an unexpected glimpse of Thomas' calm yet utterly focused sense of vocation, and of the hidden energy and depth of his personal devotion. He writes:

> Drawing confidence from God's kindness to undertake the office of a wise man, though it is an office beyond our powers, we intend so far as we can (*pro nostro modulo*) to set forth the truth professed by the Catholic faith, and to eliminate errors opposed to it. For, if I may use the words of Hilary, 'I am conscious that I owe it to God as the chief office or duty of my life that my every word (*omnis sermo meus*) and perception (*sensus*) should speak of Him.'[65]

Study and Happiness

Dedicated study in any field is a demanding discipline. But the purpose of study cannot be achieved if, when sitting down to study, students find themselves relying only on the power of grim self-will (what Simone Weil

---

[65] St Thomas Aquinas, *Summa contra Gentiles*, Bk.I, ch. II, in *Opera omnia s. Thomae Aquinatis* (Rome 1968) p. 6; cited by W. H. Principe in *Thomas Aquinas' Spirituality* (Toronto 1984) p. 14.

calls 'muscular effort'[66]). In the case of St Thomas, what explains the extraordinary driving force behind his commitment to study was, first and last, his desire to know God, and to know the things of God. Simone Weil, in an illuminating statement concerning study, composed for her Dominican friend and confidant, Fr Perrin, writes:

> The intelligence can only be led by desire. For there to be desire there must be pleasure in the work. The intelligence only grows and bears fruit in joy. The joy of learning is as indispensable in study as breathing is in running. Where it is lacking there are no real students, but only poor caricatures of apprentices who, at the end of their apprenticeship, will not even have a trade. It is the part played by joy in our studies that makes of them a preparation for spiritual life.[67]

When St Thomas speaks of 'the joy of learning' he is sometimes talking simply about the ordinary natural pleasure a student will take in a particular subject. But the profound joy of which Thomas speaks most often in his writings, and which he connects with study, has to do with the subject or object of that study, namely God. 'Contemplation [or contemplative study],' he tells us in the *Summa*, 'is delightful by reason of its object, in so far as you are contemplating what you love just as with ordinary physical seeing, which is delightful not only because the act of seeing itself is pleasurable but because you are looking at someone you love.'[68] When that

---

[66] Simone Weil, *Waiting on God* (Glasgow 1983) p. 70.
[67] *ibid.*, p. 71.
[68] ST, II II, q.180, a.7.

'someone' or that person is God, then what you begin to experience, Thomas explains – and even in some measure in this life – is a unique joy. The understanding that comes from prayerful study and contemplation is not, therefore, a cold or blind abstraction but is already, in some sense, a beginning of vision, and a joyful vision: 'As soon as you see the person you love,' Thomas notes, quoting St Gregory, 'your love for that person burns all the more intensely.'[69]

It is no accident that the word 'happy' is linked to St Thomas in the two most important early lives of the saint. '*O felix Doctor*' is a phrase we hear repeated a number of times by both William Tocco and Bernard Gui, as if 'happy teacher' were the most perfect and exact description of St Thomas as a man and a theologian.[70] Thomas tells us himself, and in a number of places, that contemplative study is 'the most delightful of all human pursuits'.[71] And he notes further that those whose lives are directed towards the pursuit of wisdom are 'the happiest anyone can be in this life'.[72] The kind of

[69] ST, II II, q.180, a.7, ad.1. For the source in Gregory, see *Homil. in Ezechielem Prophetam*, II, hom.2. PL 76, 953.

[70] See William Tocco, *Vita s. Thomae Aquinatis*, D. Prümmer (ed.), fasc.II, in *Fontes vitae s. Thomae Aquinatis*, and Bernard Gui, *Vita s. Thomae Aquinatis*, in *Fontes vitae*, fasc.III; documents edited from the *Revue thomiste*, 1913–27.

[71] St Thomas Aquinas, *Summa contra Gentiles*, Bk.I, ch. II (Rome 1918) p. 6.

[72] St Thomas Aquinas, *Sententia libri ethicorum*, Bk 10, ch. XI, 1177 b 31, in *Opera omnia sancti Thomae Aquinatis*, vol. XLVII (Roma 1969) p. 588.

happiness Thomas is describing here was manifest, we may presume, in the lives of many of the Dominicans with whom he lived and worked and studied, men of generous and passionate intelligence 'seeking the truth together,' as Albert the Great expressed it, 'in the pleasure of companionship (*in dulcedine societatis quaerere veritatem*)'.[73] Albert, in one of his sermons, speaks also of the great delight that he found, as an individual scholar, in private, dedicated research, seeking wisdom at night in the quietness of solitude: 'That enjoyment is best,' he remarked, 'which is happiest ... and that is the enjoyment which people have in their hearts with wisdom ... I have often spent the whole night like this, never suspecting that even two hours of the night had passed.'[74]

The Example of St Thomas

Already, during the lifetimes of Albert and Thomas, people expressed amazement at the depth and extent of their literary output. One witness at Thomas' canonization process remarked: 'it does not seem possible for a man using merely human powers to have written so many great works in so short a time.'[75] One part of the

[73] Albert the Great, *Politica*, Bk. 8, vi, in *Opera omnia B. Alberti*, vol. VIII (Paris 1891) p. 804.

[74] See the article by J.B. Schneyer on the sermons of Albert, in AFP XXXIV (1964) 56; cited in S. Tugwell, *Albert and Thomas*, p. 29.

[75] *Processus canonizationis s. Thomae, Napoli*, in *Fontes vitae*, M-H. Laurent (ed.), p. 384; documents edited from *Revue thomiste*, 1912–1928; trans., K. Foster O.P., in *The Life of Saint Thomas Aquinas: Biographical Documents* (London 1959) pp. 113-14.

explanation is, I would suggest, that those who really enjoy their work are almost always the most outstanding at their particular task. Thomas himself remarks that 'pleasure increases activity', and so those who find pleasure in their work, he says, 'make great progress in their own particular field'.[76] Aquinas' powers of concentration were legendary. 'It was as though the prayer of his mind never ceased,' Bernard Gui tells us, 'and in fact no external business could ever distract it from the thoughts in which he delighted.'[77] On one occasion Thomas became so absorbed in thought or meditation that he forgot where he was, ignoring completely the fact that he was seated beside an important ecclesiastical figure who had come expressly to meet him. Waking up from his trance, Thomas exclaimed: 'My Lord, please excuse me: I thought I was still in my cell. A beautiful idea has just occurred to me for the work on which I am engaged at present – a really wonderful idea it was and it gave me such pleasure!'[78]

On the subject of Thomas' dedication to study and research, there is another story, this time from Tocco, which reveals in a striking, and I think amusing, way, the emphatically intellectual character of the saint.[79] Once,

[76] St Thomas Aquinas, *Sententia libri ethicorum*, vol. X, VII, 1175 a 29, p. 572.

[77] Gui, *Vita* XV, p. 183; see also Foster, *Biographical Documents*, p. 37.

[78] Gui, *Vita*, XXV, p. 192; Foster, *Biographical Documents*, p. 45.

[79] *De visione fratris Romani*, in William Tocco, *Vita* XLV, pp. 118-19. A version of this story can also be found in Bernard Gui, *Vita* XIX, pp. 186-7.

when Thomas was praying in the Dominican convent at Naples, there appeared to him in a vision a certain Brother Romanus whom he had last seen in Paris. Romanus said to Thomas: 'I have passed from this life, but I am allowed to come to you on account of your merits.' Thomas was shaken at first by the apparition, but summoning up his courage, he said to Romanus: 'If it be pleasing to God, I adjure you by God to answer my questions.'[80] The saint then put to Romanus two rather straightforward questions, the first concerning himself, his work and the state of his soul, and the second concerning the spiritual condition of his friend. But, with the third and final question we hear, all of a sudden, breaking into the story, as it were, the voice of Friar Thomas d'Aquino, the searching, indefatigable scholar and passionate scholastic. Without any preamble, he says to Romanus: 'On that question that we have so often discussed together concerning the dispositions of knowing which we acquire here [on earth]: do they remain with us in the fatherland?'[81] It was an unexpected question to put to an apparition, and certainly not the sort of question that we imagine saints, or those who have visions of this kind, are normally inclined to ask. The answer Brother Romanus gives is short and, perhaps, not surprisingly, negative. 'Brother Thomas, I see God,' he declares, 'and you may not question me further on that subject.'[82]

---

[80] William Tocco, *Vita* XLV, p. 119.
[81] *ibid.*, p. 88.
[82] *ibid.*

111

Now that would seem to be that, with no more to be said: the end, it would appear, of a brief excursus into scholasticism. But Thomas returns at once to his point. Vision or no vision, he is a scholar with a question on his mind, and he is not going to be easily thwarted. 'Since you see God,' he says to Romanus, 'can you see Him directly, in an immediate way (*sine media specie*), or only by means of a likeness?' The ghostly visitant, at this stage, has clearly had enough. He chooses to bow out of the discussion at once and disappear, but not before delivering a short, mystical citation: 'As we have heard so we have seen in the city of our God!'[83]

For St Thomas, engagement in thought and specula-tion was never merely an intellectual pursuit. It was always part of a contemplative quest and adventure. It is no exaggeration, therefore, to say that, in Thomas' work, theology and spirituality are always one and the same thing. On this point, Torrell writes: 'If St Thomas never felt the need to develop a spirituality *alongside* his theology, that's simply because theology is itself "une *science pieuse,*" as Père Chenu loved to say.'[84] But if theology *is* for St Thomas always a contemplative task, that does not mean it became, in his life, a substitute for prayer. On the contrary, we are told by one of the early witnesses at the canonization process that 'all his writing began with prayer, and in all his difficulties he had

[83] *ibid.*, p. 89.
[84] Jean-Pierre Torrell O.P., 'Ascèse intellectuelle et vie spirituelle', *La Vie spirituelle*, 153, 733 (December 1999) 613.

recourse to prayer'.[85] Nevertheless, it has to be acknowledged that, in more than one respect, Thomas did not conform to the accepted model of a saint.[86] He was pious certainly, but he was also a man obsessed with the desire for knowledge, and with the desire to know God. And, in the end, that obsession itself was part of his holiness. A.D. Sertillanges, in his celebrated work, *La Vie intellectuelle*, writes: '[I]t is the thinker's special characteristic to be obsessed by the desire for knowledge.'[87] But study – the impulse to study – being, like prayer, rooted in *desire*, can itself become a form of prayer. Sertillanges calls it 'active prayer',[88] a way of *praying without ceasing*. And that is precisely what study became for St Thomas.

Study and Freedom

'We theologians live by the promise of Christ: "the truth will set you free"' (Jn 8:32).[89] That clear statement of vocation was made by the Dominican exegete and

[85] William Tocco was the witness. See *Processas canonizationis s. Thomae, Napoli*, LVIII, in *Fontes*, p. 346.

[86] He was not noted, for example, for working miracles. There is a story – some say a legend – that when it came to his canonization so few miracles were found in Thomas' life an objection was raised against canonizing him. But Pope John XXII intervened on behalf of the saint, remarking that every question Thomas answered was in itself a miracle. See S. Tugwell, *Albert and Thomas*, p. 259.

[87] A.D. Sertillanges O.P., *The Intellectual Life* (Cork 1965) p. 71.

[88] *ibid.*, p. 70.

[89] Dominique Barthélemy, O.P., 'The Responsibility of the Theologian', *Dominican Ashram*, X, 2 (June 1991) p. 69.

theologian Dominique Barthélemy, in an address he gave on the feast of St Albert the Great in 1990. True liberty, Barthélemy went on to explain, cannot be handed down by a fixed, juridical framework: 'It can only be gained by a demanding, patient and lucid search for the truth.'[90] No small part of the intellectual discipline to which Barthélemy is referring here is the task we call scholarship. At first sight, scholarship may seem to have little or nothing to do with spirituality or with the life of prayer. So why then should it be thought necessary? In a short but insightful paper entitled *Scholarship, Sanctity and Spirituality,* Simon Tugwell points out that 'scholarship helps to keep open or to re-open the options that are actually there in the church'.[91] He recalls the fact that Teresa of Avila always preferred learned directors to merely pious ones: 'Spiritual but unlearned directors were cramped by their own experience, they knew only one way to be Christian.' In contrast, 'Learned directors ... were more *free* precisely because of their learning, more *free* to recognise as legitimate ways of being Christian which were not part of the prevailing ethos'.[92] The reality is, of course, that people will often be swayed by the fashions of their own age. And this holds true for spirituality as for everything else. What scholarship, at its ordinary best, can help us to see is that the authentic

[90] *ibid.*, p. 80.
[91] Simon Tugwell, O.P., *Scholarship, Sanctity and Spirituality* (Spokane 1983), an address given at Gonzaga University in the United States and published in pamphlet form.
[92] *ibid.*, p. 31. Italics added.

gospel tradition is not limited by the dominant fashions of thought and feeling of one particular generation.[93]

The most notable example in Dominican history of a scholar and theologian whose work helped liberate his own and later generations from the tyranny of a single vision is St Thomas Aquinas. His first biographer, William Tocco, stresses the newness of Thomas' approach to almost everything. 'In his lectures,' Tocco writes, 'he raised *new* questions, and discovered a *new* and clear way of solving them, and he used *new* arguments in arriving at these solutions.'[94] The dominant fashion in theology, at that period, drew much of its inspiration from the Platonic and neo-Platonic traditions. But the teaching of Aristotle, in contrast, was considered a potential threat to the Christian gospel. For several years, in fact, before St Thomas arrived in Paris, there had been a ban on teaching Aristotle at the University.[95] So what was it that prompted Thomas, as a young man, to resist the dominant theological thinking

[93] This point, with respect to theology in general, was made by J.M.R. Tillard, O.P. in *Théologie et vie ecclèsiale*, in *Initiation à la pratique de la théologie*, vol. I, B. Laurent and F. Refoulé (eds) (Paris 1982) pp. 172-7. Tillard's fine paper, while giving due importance to the creative role of theology within the Church, has the merit also of indicating the differences which exist between the teaching role of scholars and theologians and that of bishops.

[94] William Tocco, *Vita*, XIV, p. 81. Italics added.

[95] Officially the ban remained in place until 1250. But, for some years before that, repeated interdictions from Rome had been largely ignored. See J-P. Torrell O.P., *Saint Thomas Aquinas: The Person and His Work* (Washington 1996) p. 38.

of his time, and open his mind to the teaching of the Greek? Why trust a source that so many revered theologians among his contemporaries considered tainted and dangerous? One answer to this question can be found in a single statement, made by St Thomas, in a letter sent to a certain Brother John, concerning study. Thomas writes: 'Do not heed by *whom* a thing is said, but rather *what* is said you should commit to memory.'[96] And, again, in another place: 'When taking up or rejecting opinions, a person should not be led by love or hate concerning who said them but rather by the certainty of truth. He [Aristotle] says we should love both kinds of people: those whose opinions we follow, and those whose opinions we reject. For both study to find the truth and, in this way, both give us assistance.'[97]

In part, as a direct result of Thomas' openness to the philosophy of Aristotle, his work fell under a cloud of suspicion for several years. Propositions taken from his work, or associated with his work, were condemned first of all by the Bishop of Paris and then later by the

[96] St Thomas Aquinas, *Epistola de modo studendi*, in *Opuscula vix dubia*, XLIV, *Opuscula omnia*, vol. IV, P. Mandonnet (ed.) (Paris 1927) p. 535. Italics added. For an assessment of the letter's authenticity, see Ch. 4, no 35 (p. 143).

[97] See St Thomas Aquinas, *Sententia super metaphysicam*, XII, 9, 2566, Marietti (ed.) (Torino 1971) p. 599. Elsewhere Thomas notes that 'any truth, no matter by whom it is said, is from the Holy Spirit (*omne verum, a quocumque dicatur, est a Spiritu Sancto*).' ST, I II, q.109, a.1, ad.1.

Archbishop of Canterbury.[98] Only after his death, in fact, was the cloud of suspicion surrounding his writings finally dispelled.[99] It is no small irony that Friar Thomas d'Aquino, the theologian and scholar who would later come to be known as *Doctor Communis* in the universal church, was at first regarded by many in the church as a sign of contradiction. Thomas himself, needless to say, was no lover of controversy for its own sake. But when, on certain occasions, the message of the gospel was at stake, he was not afraid to speak out, and to engage with others in free and open debate. Always obedient to church teaching, he was at the same time not unaware that his writings were of sufficient originality and force to provoke strong opposition from certain elements within the church. In the end, however, no amount of opposition was able to negate the quiet, purposeful witness and wisdom of his life and work.

The Freedom of Lagrange and Congar

In more recent times, a comparable shadow of suspicion fell across the writings of the Dominican exegete and theologian M.J. Lagrange. Notable for his courage and humble faith, Lagrange persisted in pursuing his research and study even though he knew it would bring him enormous suffering. To Desqueyroux he wrote, quoting

[98] See Torrell, *Saint Thomas Aquinas*, pp. 299-304. There were others, of course, during Thomas' lifetime, who actively supported and defended his work.

[99] *ibid.*, pp. 323-4.

St Jerome: 'Knowingly and prudently I put my hand into the fire (*Sciens et prudens manum misi in ignem*).'[100] What is profoundly moving, in all the writings of Lagrange during this period, is his complete surrender to the final judgment of church authority. From beginning to end he stood firm in what Barthélemy calls 'the double mission' of the theologian: 'that of maintaining freedom of theological research and that of remaining fully rooted in the midst of the church.'[101]

Yves Congar was another Dominican theologian in modern times who had to endure long and sustained opposition before the radiant truth of what he was saying became clear to everyone. At one point, exiled from Paris, and from his brethren there, and ordered to be 'silent', Congar expressed something of his distress in a letter to his 80-year-old mother. 'The French Dominicans,' he wrote, 'have been persecuted and reduced to silence ... because they were the only ones who possessed a certain freedom of thought, of enterprise and of expression. Of course, there can be no freedom without orthodoxy, but orthodoxy must also have, as its sources, the Bible, the Fathers, etc.'[102] Congar, as much as anyone in his

---

[100] M-J. Lagrange, Letter to Desqueyroux, 3 July 1901. See B. Montagnes, 'Premiers combats du p. Lagrange: la conférence de Toulouse' (1902), AFP LXI(1991) p. 358, cited in T. Radcliffe, O.P., *The Wellspring of Hope: Study and the Annunciation of the Good News*, in *Sing a New Song: The Christian Vocation* (Dublin 1999) p. 77.

[101] Barthélemy, 'The Responsibility of the Theologian', p. 68.

[102] Y. Congar O.P., 'Lettre à sa mère', in *Journal d'un théologien, 1946-1956* (Paris 2001) p. 425.

generation, understood the importance, within the church, of the freedom to think and to study, and the freedom to speak.[103] For Congar, throughout all his adult life, that freedom was part of his vocation as a scholar and a preacher, and part also of his priesthood. Study was not merely a sort of academic duty or right. It was part of a sacred trust, a commission from God to preach the Word.

In an address he delivered in 1951, Congar cited with manifest enthusiasm a passage from the work of the nineteenth-century Dominican Henri Dominique Lacordaire. Lacordaire had worked tirelessly in France for the freedom to teach – freedom for Catholics and freedom also for others. But here, in this passage, Lacordaire speaks exclusively of his own experience as a preacher of the Word: 'I never had a better grasp of freedom than on the day when, together with the blessing of the sacred oils, I received the right to speak of God. The universe then opened up before me, and I realized that in the human being there is something inalienable, divine and eternally free – the Word! The Word had been entrusted to me, as a priest, and I was told to carry it to the ends of the earth, no-one having the right to seal my lips a single day of my life.'[104]

---

[103] On 23 March, 1954, Congar made the following note in his journal: 'Dire la vérité. Prudemment, sans scandale provocant et inutile. Mais demeurer – et devenir de plus en plus – un témoin authentique et pur de ce qui est vrai. Continuer au maximum à écrire dans la même sens, utilisant toutes les chances encore libres.' *Journal*, p. 271.

[104] Cited by Y. Congar, in *La liberté dans la vie de Lacordaire*, *Les Voies du Dieu vivant: théologie et vie spirituelle* (Paris 1962) p. 337.

Study and the Neighbour

The hope of the early Dominicans was that, through their teaching and preaching, they might be 'useful to the souls of [their] neighbours'.[105] But learning, even of a theological nature, can sometimes turn in on itself, and become self-absorbed. One clear indication that the early Dominicans were determined not to let this happen, but instead to keep the focus of their attention fixed always on the neighbour, is an anecdote they took the trouble to preserve concerning Dominic. According to the report of Brother Stephen, when Dominic 'was still a student, he sold his books and fed the poor during a time of famine'.[106] The reason Dominic gave for his action is worth noting. 'I refuse,' he said, 'to study dead skins while men are dying of hunger.'[107]

The sharp awareness of human need in that statement springs not only from the tenderness of Dominic's heart but also, I suspect, from countless days and nights of

[105] Prologue, *The Early Dominican Constitutions*, in S. Tugwell, *Early Dominicans*, p. 457.

[106] *Acta canonizationis s. Dominici*, 35, p. 153

[107] *ibid.*, p. 154. Manifest in the lives of many Dominicans after the time of Dominic was an active concern for the down-trodden and the needy. Two names in particular stand out: St Martín de Porres and Bartolomé de las Casas. See Giuliana Cavallini, *St Martín de Porres: Apostle of Charity* (New York 1979), and Gustavo Gutiérrez O.P., *Las Casas: In Search of the Poor of Christ* (New York 1993). See also John Orme Mills, O.P. (ed.) *Justice, Peace and the Dominicans 1216-2001* (Dublin 2002). The intimate link between spirituality and justice is tellingly evoked by Albert Nolan O.P. in 'Spiritual Growth and the Option for the Poor', *Dominican Ashram*, V, 3 (1986) pp. 107-14.

devoted study and contemplation. Writing in the mid-thirteenth century, an anonymous Dominican at St Jacques in Paris notes that, among the things 'a man ought to see in contemplation', and ought 'to write in the book of his heart,' are 'the needs of his neighbour'.[108] And he says further: 'He ought to see [in contemplation] what he would like to have done for himself, if he were in such need.'[109] That particular understanding of the task of prayer and study has survived in the Order into modern times. Writing only a few years ago, Timothy Radcliffe, when he was Master of the Order, remarked: 'A theology that remains abstract, untouched by the sufferings of our poor violent world, has not begun its task.' And he adds: 'Let me remind you of the words of our brother Hyacinthe Cormier ... the study of "the holy books of Scripture demand of us that we acquire the entrails of mercy and extend them".'[110]

In her essay 'Reflections on the Right Use of School Studies', composed in 1942 and sent to her Dominican friend, Fr Perrin, Simone Weil notes that the effort we make to concentrate on our studies – that particular energy of attention – should help us afterwards to devote our attention to our neighbour, and especially to the neighbour whom we see to be in need. She writes: 'The useless efforts

---

[108] 'Vidit Jacob ... ': Expositio I super Apocalypsim, ch. I, edited under the name of Thomas Aquinas in Opuscula alia dubia, II, Opera omnia, vol. XXIII (Parma 1868) p. 334.

[109] ibid., p. 335.

[110] Timothy Radcliffe, O.P., 'An Integral Dominican Formation', Dominican Ashram, XIV (1995) p. 56.

made by the Curé d'Ars, for long and painful years, in his attempt to learn Latin bore fruit in the marvellous discernment which enabled him to see the very soul of his penitents behind their words and even their silences.'[111] Our struggles, and even our failures in our studies, might in the end be more valuable than our achievements. Sometimes, Aquinas tells us in the *Summa*, our own particular difficulties help us to grieve over others' misfortunes as if they were our own. Very different, he says, are those people who are always successful, 'those who regard themselves as so fortunate and powerful as to imagine that no evil can befall them: such have no pity'.[112] And he concludes: 'Thus it is always some want in us that moves us to mercy' (*semper defectus est ratio miserendi*).[113]

Already, in this chapter, attention has been given to the theme of happiness in the Dominican tradition of study. But in the *Acts* of the General Chapter of the Dominican Order held at Providence in 2001, it was stated that 'The intellectual mission of the Order calls us to share not just the "*gaudium et spes*" [the joy and hope], but also the "*luctus et angor*" [the grief and anguish] of our time.'[114]

[111] S. Weil, *Reflections on the Right Use of School Studies*, in *Waiting on God*, pp. 68-9.

[112] ST, II II, q.30, a.2; trans., by R.J. Batten, O.P., vol. 34 of the *Summa* in English translation (London 1974) p. 215.

[113] *ibid.*, p. 37.

[114] Prologue, *The Intellectual Life*, in *Acts of the Elective Chapter of the Friars of the Order of Preachers, Providence 2001*, no. 109 (Rome 2001) p. 46. A comparable statement was made in a published sermon by Albert the Great. Speaking of some awkward people, who cut themselves off from the joys and griefs of their neighbours, Albert says:

That task or mission is one which demands a particular kind of study and attention (what Simone Weil would have called 'creative attention'[115]). For not only the 'joy and hope' of our generation but also the 'grief and anguish' of the poor and oppressed are things we must write in *the book of our heart.*

Books and the Book

Learning needs books. It feeds off books. The unique conversation with the past and the present, which we call theology, is impossible without a library of some sort. For good reason, therefore, books were treated with enormous respect by the early Dominicans. 'It's astonishing,' writes Guy Bedouelle, 'to see the place books occupy in the earliest Dominican texts ... A brother was to carry neither gold nor silver, or any money; but on the other hand he might carry books, his working tools.'[116] Humbert of Romans speaks of books, in one place, as if they were hallowed objects.[117] And St Thomas, quoting

Cont.
'You should make your heart like your neighbour's heart, so that when he is happy, you are happy, and you grieve with him when he is grieving.' See the article by J.B. Schneyer containing texts of some of Albert's sermons, in *Recherches de théologie ancienne et médiévale*, 36 (1969) 121; cited in S. Tugwell, *Albert and Thomas*, p. 36.

[115] S. Weil, *Waiting on God*, pp. 105-7.

[116] See Guy Bedouelle, O.P., *Saint Dominic: The Grace of the Word*, (San Francisco 1987) p. 164.

[117] Humbert of Romans, *De libris divinis procurandis*, CXL, in *Opera de vita regulari*, vol. I, pp. 419-23.

Jerome, writes: 'Let a book never be absent from your eyes and hand.'[118]

The study undertaken by Dominicans should focus attention both on eternal things and on the natural world around us. Humbert of Romans, in his treatise on preaching, says that all creation is itself 'a book' and that 'those who know how to read this book will draw from it many things which are very serviceable for helping people to grow'.[119] But there is also a sense in which Dominicans themselves – and in particular their lives as preachers – are called to be a living text or book for others to read. Centuries before Mahatma Ghandi said so memorably, 'Let our lives be open books for all to study', a Dominican of the thirteenth century, an Englishman, had boldly suggested that the preacher's life should itself be a 'book' and that, in this book, all those who see the preacher should be able to read and study the things of God.[120]

---

[118] See St Thomas Aquinas, *Contra impugnantes Dei cultum et religionem*, XI, 2, p. A 132. St Thomas remarked, on one occasion, that he would rather possess a copy of Chrysostom on Matthew than acquire the whole of Paris. See Tocco *Vita*, XLII, p. 115.

[119] Humbert of Romans, *Treatise*, IX, 107, in S. Tugwell, *Early Dominicans*, p. 217. When speaking of creation as a book, Humbert is echoing the teaching of St Anthony of the Desert. See PL 73:1018C.

[120] *Tractatus de approbatione ordinis*, T. Käppeli (ed.), in VI (1936) pp. 148–50; cited in S. Tugwell, *The Way of the Preacher*, p. 114. It is worth noting that, on p. 150, when the 'book' is mentioned, the anonymous Dominican author takes time to speak also of the scroll or book of the prophet Ezekiel.

Dominic himself, we know, carried books with him on his journeys.[121] But, although he certainly needed books for the task of preaching, it was not on written texts alone or on learned commentaries that Dominic relied. Asked once by someone who had been particularly impressed by his learning and his preaching which books he studied most, Dominic replied that he 'studied more in the book of charity than in any other' (*in libro caritatis plus quam in alio*).[122] By the phrase 'the book of charity' Dominic is referring to the saving message of God's love revealed on the cross. In similar vein, Catherine of Siena speaks, in one of her letters, of the event of Christ's death as 'the book of life'.[123] It is, Catherine says, a truth, a revelation, written 'not with ink but with blood', and 'with such large letters' that all of us, no matter how great or small our intelligence might be, can read it easily.[124] 'This our Master,' she says, 'was raised up on the chair of the cross so that we could *study* him better.' And what we discover in this 'book of life', the truth or message that we read, is 'the eternal Father's truth, the ineffable love with which we were created'.[125]

Over a hundred years earlier, that small phrase 'the book of life' occurs in one of Jordan of Saxony's most

---

[121] Once, when crossing the Ariège river, Dominic lost his books but later they were, it seems, miraculously recovered. See *Vitae Fratrum*, II, 4, pp. 69-70.

[122] *Vitae Fratrum*, II, 25, p. 82.

[123] Letter CCCXVI, in *Le Lettere di S. Caterina da Siena*, vol. V, N. Tommasèo (ed.) (Florence 1940) p. 40.

[124] *ibid.*, p. 39.

[125] *ibid.* Italics added.

memorable letters to his great friend, the Dominican contemplative, Diana d'Andalò. What is written in 'the book of life', Jordan tells Diana, is love or charity: '[Y]ou find it written with a strange beauty when you gaze at Jesus your Saviour stretched out like a sheet of parchment on the Cross inscribed with wounds, illustrated in his own loving blood. Where else, I ask you, my dearest, is there a comparable book of love to read from?'[126] Jordan speaks of the cross as a book, but he also refers to it as a scroll (*volumen*). And it was, perhaps, that word 'scroll' which brought to his mind, all of a sudden, the passage in Ezekiel in which the prophet is commanded by God to 'eat the book' or 'eat the scroll'. In any case, Jordan at once begins to connect the 'writing' or message of the cross of Christ with the scroll of Ezekiel. For Jordan the cross is nothing other than the new 'book of life'. It is the final scroll we have been given by God to read and study. And so he says to Diana:

> Turn this book over, open it, read it; you will find in it what the prophet found: lamentations, song and woe.[127] Lamentations, because of the pains which he endured;

[126] Letter XV, in *Beati Iordani de Saxonia Epistolae*, MOPH XXIII, A. Walz O.P. (ed.) (Rome 1951) p. 17; trans. S. Tugwell *Early Dominicans*, p. 405.

[127] In Ezekiel 2:10, the words on the scroll are 'lamentations, wailings and woe'. But in the Latin (Vulgate) translation, which was available to Jordan of Saxony, the second word was not translated as 'wailings' but as 'song' (*carmen*): '*lamentationes, et carmen, et vae*.' This reading or mis-reading in the Vulgate enabled Jordan to introduce into his letter the theme of Christ's 'song of gladness'.

a song of gladness, which he won for you by his pains; and the woe of unending death, from which he redeemed you by his death. In his lamentation learn to have patience in yourself, learn love in his song of joy, because surely he has the first claim on your love, seeing that he wanted you to be a sharer in such great joys. And when you realize that you have been rescued from that woe, what else should result but thanksgiving and the sound of praise?[128]

Although, for the discipline of theology, we need to read many books, what we will gain in the end is mere information unless we begin, as students of the gospel, to turn over in our minds and read and study what Dominic and Jordan and Catherine called 'the book of life' or 'the book of love'. One of the sure signs that we have begun, in an authentic way, to read and study theology is when our reading and study lead us not only to new knowledge and information concerning the gospel but also to a new depth of wonder and praise, a new song of thanksgiving.

[128] Jordan of Saxony, Letter XV, MOPH XXIII, p. 17; S. Tugwell, *Early Dominicans*, p. 405.

4

Dominicans Drinking: Preachers and the New Wine of the Gospel

One image which recurs in the writings of the early Dominican preachers, and in the stories they liked to tell about themselves, is the image or the metaphor of drinking. Of course this image has often been used by Christians and non-Christians, over the centuries, in order to evoke aspects of their religious life and experience.[1] But Dominicans seem to have taken to this metaphor with a distinctive enthusiasm, and to have used it in a great variety of ways. Thus, in their writings, the image of drinking or of being made drunk describes not only the overwhelming impact the Word of God has had on their interior lives, but also the effect of that encounter on almost every other aspect of their lives as preachers.

[1] See Aimé Solignac, 'Ivresse spirituelle', in *Dictionnaire de spiritualité*, vol. VII (Paris 1971) pp. 2312-37.

In this chapter my intention is, first of all, to examine the way the image of drinking or drunkenness was used by Jordan of Saxony, Dominic's successor as Master of the Order, and by some of the early friars. Then I will reflect on the use of the image in the work of St Thomas Aquinas. And, finally, I will examine some of the ways it was taken up and used in the writings of three Dominican mystics, St Catherine of Siena, Meister Eckhart and Johannes Tauler.[2]

1. Jordan of Saxony and 'the Wine of Hope'

(a) Drunk on New Wine

More perhaps than any of the early Dominicans, Jordan of Saxony was fond of the image of drinking. We find it recurring, for example, in a number of his sermons which have survived. On one occasion, preaching with characteristic vigour, Jordan speaks of 'the strength of wine' which, he notes, 'gives a person a lift' (*facit ... salire*) because 'wine brings delight and puts a man at his ease'

---

[2] Little or no attention, to my knowledge, has been given to this subject before now. The only paper of interest I have been able to discover is a short article by Giacinto D'Urso O.P. devoted exclusively to the work of St Catherine of Siena. See *L'Ebrezza spirituale (o sobria ebrietas) in S. Caterina*, in T. Centi, O.P. (ed.) *S. Caterina tra i dottori della chiesa* (Florence 1970) pp. 103-14. Another study by Mario Ismaele Castellano O.P. is entitled *Il vino, la bibbia e santa Caterina* (*Quaderni Cateriniani* 52-3). In spite, however, of its promising title, only two pages of the work are devoted to Catherine.

(*vinum enim facit levem et iocundum*).[3] This idea is repeated in another sermon (no. 20) where, after a brief, memorable reference to 'the wine of hope' we hear once again of '[the] good wine which,' according to the preacher, 'puts a man at his ease, gives him a lift, and stops him feeling his sorrows' (*vinum facit hominem levem et salire et dolores non sentire*).[4] The preacher of this second sermon is, according to the scholar Franco Morenzoni, once again Blessed Jordan of Saxony. Morenzoni says this because the same joyous statement about wine is repeated in both sermons (in almost the same words) and because there is no doubt whatever about the attribution of the first sermon to Jordan.[5]

The image of drinking also occurs in a few of the letters Jordan wrote to his great friend, the contemplative nun, Diana d'Andolò. Diana was sometimes undergoing very severe trials, and Jordan, writing to try to console her,

[3] Sermon 11: *In festo sancti Ioannis, die 27 decembris*, in *Beati Iordani de Saxonia: Sermones*, Paul-Bernard Hodel O.P. (ed.) MOPH XXIX (Rome 2005) p. 114. The sermons of Jordan have not survived in texts composed and edited by Jordan himself, but in the form of *reportationes*, reports or versions of the sermons noted down by others.

[4] Sermon 20: *Cum esset desponsata mater Ihesu*, in Hodel, *Sermones* p. 19. The same sermon is listed as number 43 by Franco Morenzoni in *Les Sermons de Jourdain de Saxe, successeur de saint Dominique*, AFP, LXVI, (1996), p. 205.

[5] Morenzoni places the second sermon (Sermon 43 in his listing) under 'sermons whose attribution [to Jordan] can now be confirmed'. See Morenzoni, *Sermons* pp. 205 and 229. Hodel places it (Sermon 20 in his listing) under the rubric 'other anonymous sermons which could be attributed to Jordan of Saxony'. See Hodel, *Sermones* pp. 17-18.

says in one of his letters that a time will come when she will be rewarded by Christ for her faithfulness, 'when no tribulation shall any longer come to you, but together we shall drink of the pure and unmixed chalice of everlasting joy'.[6] Jordan returns to this theme in another letter, remarkable for its comforting vision and great tenderness.[7] In contrast to the inevitable suffering we undergo in this world, Jordan speaks of the great joy awaiting us in heaven. And, in order to describe this joy, he makes use, over and over again, of the image of wine, repeating, as it happens, some of the words and phrases used in the homily referred to above (no. 20). There, reference is made not only to the 'wine of hope' but also to 'the wine of joy' and to 'the wine which makes man's heart glad'.[8] In the end, the preacher says, when all fear is gone and hope finds its fulfilment, then 'we will drink that new wine which no earthly vessel can contain'.[9] In his letter to Diana, Jordan strikes again the note of encouragement and joy but, this time, with an even more vivid, more moving eloquence. At 'the wedding-feast of the Lamb,' he writes,

[6] *Epistola XXVI*, in *Beati Iordani de Saxonia epistulae*, A. Walz O.P., (ed.), MOPH XXIII (Rome 1951) p. 30; translated in *To Heaven with Diana: A Study of Jordan of Saxony and Diana d'Andalò with a translation of the Letters of Jordan*, G. Vann O.P. (ed.) (London 1960) p. 117.

[7] *Epistola XXXV*, Walz, *Epistulae* pp. 41-2.

[8] Sermon 20: *Cum esset desponsata mater Ihesu*, Hodel, *Sermones*, pp. 19, 21.

[9] *ibid.*, p. 19.

[the Lamb] will give sweet wine to those whose soul is
suffering bitterness through thirst of love; he will wipe up
the water of this sad and savourless life and replace it by the
holy and fruitful wine, that noble wine, the wine which
makes man's heart glad, that wine with whose sweetness the
beloved of God are inebriated, I mean the wine of everlasting
joy: the rare wine, the new wine which the Son of God,
blessed for ever, pours out for his elect at the table of the
court of heaven.[10]

Unfortunately, none of the letters of Diana have
survived, so we can only guess at the impact which a
letter like the one just quoted above made on the
recipient. But we do know, from Jordan himself, the effect
another letter had on a woman living in Cologne. It was
sent, not by Jordan, but by Jordan's great friend, Henry of
Cologne. Henry, in his letter, had recommended apparently that this person 'recline on the breast of Jesus,' and
there 'quench the thirst' of her soul. 'These words
inflamed her,' Jordan informs us, and she experienced
such ecstasy, that 'she became quite drunk with the
enormous flow of well-being which she felt.' It was some
time, Jordan then goes on to say, before 'the intoxicating
spiritual sweetness left her'.[11]

[10] *Epistola* XXXV, in Walz, *Epistulae* pp. 41-2; translated by K.
Pound in *Love among the Saints: The Letters of Blessed Jordan of Saxony
to Blessed Diana of Andalò* (London 1959) p. 17.
[11] Jordan of Saxony, *Libellus de Principiis Ordinis Praedicatorum*,
85, in MOPH XVI, M.H. Laurent O.P. (ed.), (Roma 1935) pp. 65-6;
translated in S. Tugwell, *Jordan of Saxony: On the Beginnings of the
Order of Preachers*, p. 21.

According to this account by Jordan, the focus of attention is on our human thirst for God. But, in a homily which he preached in England in 1229, Jordan changes the focus of attention to God's thirst for us. And the statement he makes is as profound as it is surprising. Jordan starts off, characteristically, speaking in a very down-to-earth, colloquial manner: 'Nowadays people say, "I think it would be great if you could come to me and have a drink with me." And it's just like that with the Lord. For he says to the soul: "Give me something to drink." O if only you knew the love of God which is saying to you, "I thirst"!'[12]

At one of the earliest Chapters of the Order, being apparently much too sick to give an address, Jordan was asked instead 'to say a few words of consolation'.[13] In his brief speech, he drew the attention of his brethren to one particular sentence from the Acts of the Apostles: 'They were all filled with the Holy Spirit.' The sentence occurs in that passage in Chapter 2 of Acts, in which the apostles at Pentecost are accused of being drunk: 'They have been drinking too much new wine,' some of the bystanders sneered. (Acts 2:13) But St Peter spoke out at once in their defence: 'No, they are not drunk,' he exclaimed. And, of course, he was right. Nevertheless, something extraordinary *had* happened. These first preachers, as was indicated earlier in the same passage, had become 'filled' *not* with wine, but 'with the Holy Spirit'.

[12] Sermon 11: *In festo sancti Ioannis, die 27 decembris*, in Hodel, *Sermones*, p. 113.

[13] *Vitae Fratrum*, III, 42, xii, B.M. Reichert O.P. (ed.) (Louvain 1846) p. 142.

In his own short address, Jordan of Saxony, in spite of failing health, spoke to his brethren of the fullness of life and grace given to those who are poor in spirit. And to make his point vivid, he used the image of a goblet or a drinking-cup filled to overflowing. 'My brothers, during this week [of Pentecost] we often say these words, "They were all filled with the Holy Spirit." You know that a drinking-cup, once it is full, can hold no more. All that is poured in, only flows out again. On this account the holy apostles were filled with the Holy Spirit having been first emptied of their own spirit.'[14] In a sense, therefore, the accusation made in Acts against the first preachers at Pentecost was not inaccurate. They *were* 'drunk' or 'filled with new wine'. But they were drunk on the 'new wine' of the Gospel.

(b) Getting Others Drunk

The idea of somehow getting others 'drunk' through preaching is an idea which also appealed to Blessed Humbert of Romans. In his treatise on preaching, in a section entitled *The Usefulness of Preaching*, Humbert writes: 'there are wines so weak that they cannot intoxicate. But the Word of God is like a strong wine and it does intoxicate.'[15] He quotes Jeremiah: 'I became like a man who is drunk, like someone sodden with wine, from my encounter with

---

[14] *ibid.*, p. 142.

[15] Humbert of Romans, *Treatise on the Formation of Preachers*, 70, in S. Tugwell O.P., *Early Dominicans: Selected Writings* (New York 1982) p. 202.

the words of God' (Jer. 23:9). Humbert understands very well from experience that often it is from the roused enthusiasm and awakened faith of God's people listening to the Word that the preacher himself catches fire. He quotes Proverbs: 'He who makes others drunk will himself be made drunk too' (Prov. 11:25). And Humbert adds: 'The gloss on this says: "The one who makes his hearers drunk with the words of God will himself be made drunk with a draft of manifold blessing." '[16]

One of the early witnesses of the Order's beginnings, Brother Stephen, says of Dominic that 'he had never heard anyone whose words moved the brethren so much to compunction and weeping'.[17] And Dominic himself often wept – not only when he was preaching, but also during Mass at the moment just before the consecration of the wine. According to Brother John of Bologna who often assisted Dominic at Mass, 'tears were often flowing from his eyes when he turned to take the wine … after receiving the Lord's Body'.[18] Here the two central realities in Dominic's life are clearly manifest: the wine of Christ's blood which he drank, and the wine of Christ's Word which he preached.

Other Dominicans of the first and second generations were also noted for the passion of their preaching. As a

[16] ibid., no. 34; S. Tugwell, Early Dominicans, p. 195. See also no.176; S. Tugwell, Early Dominicans, p. 237, and no.325; S. Tugwell, Early Dominicans, pp. 272-3.

[17] 'Bologna Canonization Process, 37', trans., S. Tugwell, in K. Kondelka, Dominic (London 1997) p. 138.

[18] Vitae Fratrum, II, 18, p. 79; Koudelka, Dominic, p. 88.

direct result of hearing Blessed Reginald of Orleans preach in Paris, for example, Jordan of Saxony joined the Order. In his *Libellus* Jordan says of Reginald: 'His fervent eloquence fired the hearts of all who heard it as if it had been a blazing torch; hardly anyone was rock-like enough to be proof against its heat. The whole of Bologna was in ferment.'[19] This kind of intense emotional fervour was clearly not uncommon among the very early friars. But when later Dominicans, such as Humbert of Romans, came to write *about* preaching and other aspects of the Gospel, they tended to write in a much more dispassionate and intellectual manner. This tendency found its most notable expression in the work of St Thomas who was, in fact, writing when Humbert was Master.

In subsequent centuries, we have come to identify the Dominican approach, at its ordinary best, with the grace of a serene, intellectual objectivity. But it should be noted that a distinctly passionate fervour in preaching was at least as much a characteristic of the early Dominicans. Among the most famous of all the early preachers in the Order was Jordan of Saxony himself. According to the ancient account, he 'overflowed with enthusiastic talk, brilliant with apt and powerful illustrations'.[20] And he quite consciously worked at getting his hearers 'drunk' on the Word. Once, when he was preaching at Padua, someone asked him why he had such manifest success

[19] Jordan of Saxony, *Libellus*, 58, p. 53; trans., S. Tugwell, *Jordan of Saxony: On the Beginnings of the Order of Preachers*, p. 15.

[20] *Vitae Fratrum*, III, 11, p. 108; trans., S. Tugwell, *Early Dominicans*, p. 127.

with the arts students, the students of Aristotle, but seemed to make little impact on the theologians and canonists. Jordan replied, speaking with characteristic verve and good humour:

> Arts men drink the plain water of Aristotle and the other philosophers all week. So when they are offered the words of Christ or his disciples in a Sunday sermon or on a feast-day, they fall victim at once to the intoxication of the Holy Spirit's wine, and hand over to God not only their goods but themselves. But these theologians are always listening to the words of God, and they go the same way as a country sacristan who passes the altar so often that he loses his reverence for it and frequently turns his back on it, while outsiders bow reverently towards it.[21]

As a direct result of listening to Jordan, an amazing number of young men joined the Dominican Order. They had obviously become intoxicated with 'the Spirit's wine'. But Jordan's unique genius or 'tactic' with respect to vocations was not always matched by the recruitment practice of some the brethren. One report indicates that actual alcohol may have been employed, on one occasion, to 'encourage' a particular individual to join the Order! The source for this account is a letter sent by Pope Innocent IV in 1244. At that time there was, apparently, at least the suspicion that a number of friars actually got a schoolmaster from Asti drunk, and then forced a habit on

---

[21] Jordan of Saxony, *Libellus*, III, 42, ix, p. 141; trans., S. Tugwell, *Early Dominicans*, p. 130.

him[22] – not, obviously, the kind of *spiritual* intoxication Jordan of Saxony had in mind!

2. St Thomas Aquinas and 'the Wine of Wisdom'

We do not tend to associate Thomas Aquinas with the idea of drunkenness. We regard him rather – and for good reason – as a very brilliant, but sober, intellectual. Thomas, however, no less than Jordan of Saxony, uses the image of drinking or of drunkenness to explore some of the most basic aspects of Christian and Dominican experience. 'Wine,' he notes in his commentary on Boethius' *De Trinitate*, 'often signifies divine wisdom,' whereas 'water signifies secular wisdom.'[23] St Thomas, in his own work as a theologian, draws again and again on the wisdom of secular, non-Christian sources, a fact which disturbed more than a few of his own contemporaries. Was there not a danger, they wondered, that such reliance on secular knowledge would in some way water down the great wine of God's teaching? Thomas confronted this question head on, and answered it with what would seem to be an allusion to Christ's first miracle at Cana in Galilee. Human learning in itself is not, according to Thomas, the problem. If teachers make accurate use of 'the water' of secular knowledge, they do not so much 'mix water with wine', Thomas argues, but

---

[22] Letter of Innocent IV, in *Registrum*, no.529. See S. Tugwell, *Early Dominicans*, p. 154, n.27.

[23] St Thomas Aquinas, *Super Boethium de Trinitate*, q.2, a.3, ad.5 (Rome 1992) p. 97.

rather change the water of human learning into the wine of Gospel truth.[24]

(a) Water into Wine: The Miracle at Cana

Christ's visit to Cana – the joy of that visit – signifies for St Thomas, 'the effect of God's words on our minds'. For these words, he says, cause delight and joy. And 'this is signified in the miracle of the wine, which, as the Psalm (103:15) says, "gladdens the heart of man."' This observation concerning joy occurs in Thomas' commentary on St John's Gospel.[25] It seems to parallel a statement made, centuries later, in Fyodor Dostoevsky's novel *The Brothers Karamazov*. Alyosha, the youngest of the brothers, hearing this particular text being read from the Gospel, exclaims: 'I love that passage; it's Cana in Galilee, the first miracle ... Ah, that miracle, what a lovely miracle! It wasn't sorrow, it was human happiness that Christ extolled, and the first miracle he worked was to bring men happiness.'[26] Of course, Thomas' concern in his commentary is not with the natural effects of ordinary wine, but with the supernatural effects of the new wine of the Gospel. He is interested here not so much in the literal meaning of the text, but in what he calls 'the mystical sense'.

[24] *ibid.*, p. 100.

[25] St Thomas Aquinas, *Commentary on the Gospel of John* (Jn 4:46) no. 674, trans., J.A. Weisheipl, O.P. (New York) p. 271. See also Thomas' commentary on Jn 2:1-11, nos.334-65, pp. 149-59.

[26] F. Dostoyevsky, *The Brothers Karamazov* (New York 1972), p. 436.

One can find no reference in this section of St John's Gospel to preachers or to preaching. But Thomas cannot resist bringing in the subject. And he does this with a quite unembarrassed sleight of hand, employing the rubric of 'the mystical sense'. The text in question is Jesus' request to the servants 'to pour out some drink and bring it to the head waiter' (Jn. 2:8). 'In the mystical sense,' Thomas tells us, 'those who pour out the water are preachers.'[27] He quotes Isaiah: 'With joy you will draw water from the spring of the Saviour' (Isa. 12:3). And then he goes on to say that: 'When the word of the Gospel, which was hidden under the letter of the law, is entrusted to preachers, it is as though wine made from water is poured out.'[28] The link between wine and the spirit of the Gospel seems to be instinctive in Thomas. His commentary, for example, on the small phrase, 'They have no wine' (Jn. 2:4), draws out with such plain eloquence and profound insight the differences between the Old Law and the New, that I cannot resist quoting it here at some length.

> *They have no wine.* Here we should note that before the Incarnation of Christ three wines were running out: the wine of justice, of wisdom, and of charity or grace. Wine stings, and in this respect it is a symbol of justice. But wine also delights the heart, 'Wine cheers the heart of man' (Ps. 103:15). And in this respect wine is a symbol of wisdom, the meditation of which is enjoyable in the highest degree:

[27] St Thomas Aquinas, *Commentary on the Gospel of John*, no. 361, p. 157.

[28] *ibid.*, p. 157.

140

'Her companionship has no bitterness' (Wis. 8:16).
Further, wine intoxicates: 'Drink, friends, and be intoxicated, my dearly beloved' (Song 5:1). And in this respect
wine is a symbol of charity ... The wine of justice was
indeed running out in the old law, in which justice was
imperfect. But Christ brought it to perfection: 'Unless your
justice is greater than that of the scribes and of the
Pharisees, you will not enter into the kingdom of heaven'
(Mt. 5:20). The wine of wisdom was also running out, for it
was hidden and symbolic ... but Christ clearly brought
wisdom to light: 'He was teaching them as one having
authority' (Mt. 7:9). The wine of charity was also running
out, because they had received a spirit of serving only in
fear. But Christ converted the water of fear into the wine of
love (*aquam timoris ... in vinum caritatis*) when he gave us
'the spirit of adoption as sons by which we cry: "Abba,
Father"' (Rom. 8:15).[29]

(b) Drunk on Wisdom

'Drink, friends, and be intoxicated!' This astonishing
imperative from the Song of Songs, which Thomas
quoted in his commentary on St John's Gospel, is taken
up and quoted again in his commentary on Psalm 35.
But, this time, with an unexpected vividness, Thomas
speaks of the force of the torrent of God's Spirit within
the soul. It is, he says, of such force at times that there is
no way it can be resisted. 'And just as those who hold
their mouths to the fountain of wine become drunk or
inebriated, likewise those who bring their desires, or hold

---

[29] *ibid.*, no.347, p. 153.

their mouths, as it were, to the fountain of life and sweetness, become drunk [in the spirit].'[30]

Thomas returns to this theme in the *Summa* where he notes, with a single telling phrase, that 'just as material wine inebriates *literally* [i.e. makes the person physically drunk] likewise meditation on wisdom is metaphorically speaking [i.e. at the level of the spirit] an intoxicating drink.'[31] In another place, also in the *Summa*, Thomas repeats again the happy imperative, 'Eat, O friends, and drink, and be inebriated.' But this time the phrase occurs in a section where Thomas is reflecting on the love of God poured out for us in the Eucharist. 'The love of God,' he says, quoting St Gregory the Great, 'is never idle.' For 'wherever it is, it does great works.' And so, by allowing ourselves to drink in God's love in the Eucharist, we become 'spiritually gladdened and are, as it were, inebriated with the sweetness of the divine Goodness'.[32]

Wine, in St Thomas' opinion, is an illuminating symbol of 'divine teaching' and also, therefore, of wisdom: first, 'because wine pierces by uncovering things,' second, 'because it inflames by exhorting,' and third, 'because it intoxicates by consoling, as in [the text of] Isaiah, "You

---

[30] St Thomas Aquinas, *Postilla super Psalmos,* 35, in *Expositio in aliquot libros veteris Testamentis, Opera omnia,* vol. XIV (Parma 1863) p. 278. Thomas refers again to Psalm 35 in the Prologue to his *Commentary on the Sentences of Peter Lombard.* There he says that Christ, with his 'abundant fruitfulness,' will make the blessed in heaven *inebriated.* And he adds: 'It is called drunkenness because it passes beyond all measure of reason and desire.'

[31] ST, II II, q.149, a.1, ad.1. Italics added.

[32] ST, III, q.79, a.1, ad.2.

are becoming drunk from the abundance of your consolation." [33] This brief passage from Thomas' commentary on Isaiah makes it abundantly clear that he is in no way opposed to the passionate fervour – the 'inebriation' to use his own word – which forms part of living faith. That said, however, in his work as theologian and teacher, Thomas much prefers to describe this state with clarity and serenity rather than to manifest it.

(c) St Dominic and St Thomas

In order to grasp the full significance of St Thomas' achievement, it is imperative to see him within his own historical context, and see him in relation particularly to St Dominic and to the Friars Preachers. Owing to Thomas' enormous intellectual presence in the history of the Church, there has been a tendency over the years (and especially, perhaps, among theologians) to regard him as a figure of such unique and 'angelic' authority as almost to transcend history altogether. But Thomas' own passionate commitment to the intellectual life sprang, first and last, from his vocation as a Friar Preacher and from his commitment, therefore, to serve the Gospel at a particular time and in a particular place. The one indisputable reference which Thomas makes to Dominic is hardly known, and is almost never quoted. It occurs in one of Thomas' homilies in which St Dominic and his contemporary, St Francis of Assisi, are described as

[33] St Thomas Aquinas, *Expositio super Isaiam ad litteram*, 55, 103-8, in *Opera omnia*, XXVIII (Rome 1974) p. 222.

'glorious ministers' appointed by God for the salvation of men and women, ministers who made it their special care (*speciale studium*) to 'lead people to salvation'.[34]

There is another brief reference to St Dominic in a work entitled *De modo studendi* which, for hundreds of years, has been attributed to St Thomas.[35] The letter is addressed to a young Dominican called Brother John, who had sought guidance from the Master precisely on the question of study. In Thomas' reply, Brother John is encouraged not only to devote himself to study, but also to look out beyond the world of academe to the wider world and to its needs (i.e. to what Thomas calls 'the Lord's vineyard'), and there 'to follow in the footsteps of Blessed Dominic'.[36] Study is to be pursued – yes – but always with a view to building up God's kingdom here and now. Thomas says of Dominic that, in the vineyard of the Lord, he produced things not only 'useful' but also

[34] St Thomas Aquinas, '*Homo quidam erat dives: Sermo in Dominica IX post festum Trinitatis*', in *Index thomisticus: S. Thomae Aquinatis Opera omnia*, vol. 6, no.6, 2, R. Busa (ed.) (Stuttgart-Bad Cannstatt 1980) p. 38.

[35] '*Epistola de modo studendi*', in *Opuscula vix dubia*, XLIV, Opuscula omnia, vol. IV, P. Mandonnet (ed.) (Paris 1927) p. 535. Although the historical grounds for the letter's authenticity are by no means conclusive, James Weisheipl O.P. notes that, 'its authenticity has been tentatively accepted by all scholars since Quetif-Echard'. See J. Weisheipl O.P., *Friar Thomas D'Aquino: His Life, Thought, and Works* (Washington 1983) pp. 397–8. See also Victor White O.P., 'The Letter of St Thomas to Brother John *De modo studendi*', *Life of the Spirit: Blackfriars*, (1944 suppl.) pp. 161–80.

[36] *ibid.*

'wonderful', bringing forth and increasing 'buds, flowers and fruits'.[37] (In parenthesis here, it may be of some interest to place alongside this image of exuberant growth and fullness of life a saying which Pope John XXIII loved to repeat: 'We are not here on earth as museum keepers, but to cultivate a flourishing garden of life.'[38])

(d) Preachers Open to the World

Thomas, in his letter on study, refers at one point to what he calls 'the wine-cellar [of wisdom]'. 'Do not neglect prayer,' he writes, 'and remain often in your cell if you wish to be admitted to the wine-cellar.'[39] With these words, St Thomas does not mean to encourage Brother John to turn his back on all life and thought outside the cloister. In fact, Thomas goes on almost at once to encourage his brother Dominican to remain open to truth wherever he meets it. 'Do not be concerned,' he notes, 'about what speaker you are listening to; instead when something good is said, commit it to memory.'[40] St Thomas develops this point elsewhere in his work. In his commentary on the *Metaphysics* of Aristotle, for example, he writes: 'When taking up or rejecting opinions a person should not be led by love or hate concerning who said

[37] *ibid.*

[38] This Pope John called one of his 'favourite phrases'. See Peter Hebblethwaite, *Pope John XXIII: Pope of the Council* (London 1984) p. 269.

[39] '*Epistola de modo studendi*,' p. 535.

[40] *ibid.*

145

them but only by the certitude of truth. [Aristotle] says we should love both kinds of people: those whose opinions we follow, and those whose opinions we reject. For both study to find the truth and in this way they are our helpers.'[41]

The radiant openness to truth and the inspired humanism of these statements clearly reflect something of St Thomas' own distinctive genius and character. But they represent also, I would say, something of the Christian humanist tradition which Thomas inherited from his own brethren, the Friars Preachers. At one point in the *Vitae Fratrum*, the Dominicans - these 'new-comers'[42] - are said to be not only bearers of the 'wine' of Gospel truth, but also gatherers of the 'honey' of human wisdom and learning. The text itself says that they are 'dispensers of the wine and honey, since they blend in their preaching the sweetness of divine things with the pleasantness of human learning'.[43] And, when they 'mix the honey with the wine, and pour wine upon the honey, and [give] it to the people to drink,' the effect is something great. In the symbolic words of one ecstatic account, those among the people who take this new drink, begin 'to run to and fro as if beside themselves with its sweetness'.[44]

[41] See St Thomas Aquinas, *Sententia super metaphysicam*, XII, 2566 (Torino 1950) p. 599.

[42] *Vitae Fratrum*, I, 4 vii, p. 22; trans., Placid Conway in *Lives of the Brethren*, (London 1955) p. 11.

[43] *ibid.*, pp. 22-3, n.17; P. Conway, *Lives*, p. 11.

[44] *ibid.*, pp. 22-3. See also p. 22, n. 17.

One story about actual wine-drinking which involves St Dominic himself is recorded in the *Miracula* composed by Blessed Cecilia.[45] Apparently, Dominic arrived late one night with some of his brethren to visit a particular convent of the sisters. The nuns had already retired to bed. But when the bell was rung – the known signal for the preacher's arrival – they all got up from their beds at once and came down to the church. There Dominic delivered what is described by Blessed Cecilia as a 'long conference'. The text, however, adds that it 'brought them great consolation'. And then, the text continues:

> When he had finished speaking, he said, 'It would be good, my daughters, to have something to drink.' He called brother Roger, the cellarer, to bring some wine and a cup ... Then he blessed it and drank from it himself ... After the brethren had all had a drink, St Dominic said: 'I want all my daughters to have a drink' ... Then all the sisters drank from it ... and they all drank as much as they wanted, encouraged by St Dominic, who kept on saying, 'Drink up, my daughters!' At that time there were 104 sisters there, and they all drank as much wine as they wanted.[46]

My favourite image of St Dominic is one painted on wood, which can be seen in Bologna. It records 'the miracle of bread' which, according to tradition, took place at the convent of Santa Maria alla Mascerella. In this medieval work, Dominic's contemplative identity is indicated by the black capuce over his head. But the

---

[45] Blessed Cecilia, *Miracula*, 6. See S. Tugwell, *Early Dominicans*, pp. 391–2.

[46] *ibid*.

man we see before us is, first and last, 'vir evangelicus', a man 'in persona Christi' surrounded by his brethren, and seated at table, at a meal, which as well as recalling 'the miracle of bread' at once suggests a communal and liturgical life, a real eucharistic fellowship. His look is one of extraordinary candour, and his physical presence gives the impression of a man of robust simplicity, a man entirely at ease with himself and with the world around him. In all of medieval iconography, I can think of no other religious painting or fresco in which a saint is shown, as here, looking out at the world with such serene confidence and ease of spirit.

One small detail worth noting is the way Dominic's right hand takes hold of the bread so decisively, while his left hand, no less firm and strong, holds on to the table. This image of St Dominic in paint bears no resemblance whatever to that caricature of the Christian spirit which Friedrich Nietzsche put forward in his book *The Anti-Christ*. There, the Christian spirit is described as 'a condition of morbid susceptibility of the *sense of touch* which makes it shrink back in horror from every contact, every grasping of a firm object'.[47] But the Dominic of this painting, like the Dominic of history, in fact possessed a very firm and very vital hold on the immediate world around him.

That sense of openness to the world is a marked characteristic of many of the great Dominican preachers. 'When I became a Christian,' noted Lacordaire, 'I did not

[47] Nietzsche, *The Anti-Christ* (Harmondsworth 1968) p. 141.

lose sight of the world.'[48] And, in the twentieth century, Vincent McNabb remarked once to some of his brethren: 'The world is waiting for those who love it ... If you don't love men don't preach to them – preach to yourself'![49]

One of the most striking observations ever made about God's love for the world occurs in St Matthew's Gospel. Chapter 11 is made by Jesus himself, and it throws into immediate and stark relief the newness of the way which Jesus chose to relate to sinners. I find this passage uniquely memorable because of the contrast suggested between the seeming 'ordinariness' of Jesus – a man 'eating and drinking' – and the austere, extraordinary figure of John the Baptist: 'For John came neither eating nor drinking, and they say, "He has a demon"; the Son of man came eating and drinking, and they say, "Behold, a glutton and a drunkard, a friend of tax collectors and sinners"!' (Mt 11:18-19). This particular chapter in St Matthew's Gospel received notable attention from St Thomas in his commentary on the Gospel. 'John [the Baptist],' he writes, 'chose the way of austerity (*viam austeritatis*) but the Lord chose for himself a way of gentleness (*viam lenitatis*).'[50] And what is more, 'John marked the end of the Old Testament in which grave [matters] were imposed. But

[48] Henri Dominique Lacordaire, *Notice*, p. 43, cited by Yves Congar O.P. in *Faith and Spiritual Life* (London 1969) p. 106.

[49] Spoken by McNabb during a retreat in 1927. See *An Old Apostle Speaks: Father Vincent McNabb O.P.*, G. Vann O.P. (ed.) (Oxford 1946) p. 3.

[50] St Thomas Aquinas, *Lectura super Matthaeum*, XI, in *Opera omnia*, X (Parma 1861) p. 111.

149

Christ marked the beginning of the New Law, which proceeds by the way of clemency.'[51] Compared with St John, 'Christ assumed a more human life',[52] which means he accepted living a social life. 'The human being,' Thomas says, 'is naturally social.'[53] And, what is more, as human beings we incline instinctively to what delights us or gives us pleasure (*naturale est homini quaerere delectationes*).[54] In parenthesis here, it is worth noting that, in the *Summa*, Thomas declares: 'No one can live without any sensate or physical pleasure.' And he adds: 'the very man who teaches that all pleasure is evil is bound to be caught taking some pleasure.'[55] That said, however, St. Thomas is well aware that, all too quickly, we can be drawn into 'harmful pleasures'.[56] Clearly, therefore, there is need for a radical discipline of some kind. Nevertheless, for Thomas, good company and the ordinary delights of food and drink are never evil in themselves.[57] He quotes Eccl. 40:20, 'Wine and music delight the heart'. And he quotes also what is surely Aristotle's most brilliant aphorism: 'Anyone who doesn't need company (*solitarius*) is either

[51] *ibid.*
[52] *ibid.*
[53] *ibid.*, p. 110.
[54] *ibid.*
[55] ST, I II, q.34, a.1.
[56] St Thomas Aquinas, *Lectura super Matthaeum*, XI, p. 110.
[57] On one occasion, according to Tolomeo of Lucca, St Thomas, in gratitude to St Agnes for a certain favour received, declared that he would like to give his students a good dinner in honour of her feast-day, every year! See Tolomeo, XXIII, 10, as cited in J-P Torrell O.P., *Initiation à saint Thomas d'Aquin* (Paris 1993) pp. 396-7.

greater than a man, and is a God, or lesser than a man, and is a beast'![58]

St Thomas' vision of the world, while owing a considerable debt to Aristotle, is also uniquely indebted to the witness of his brothers in the Order, to St Dominic in particular, and to Dominic's Christian understanding of the goodness of creation. Although never naive, Thomas' vision is, at times, so impressively open and relaxed, it provoked Josef Pieper, on one occasion, to speak of it as a theologically-founded *worldliness*![59] 'It was as a theologian,' Pieper notes, 'that Thomas cast his choice for the worldliness represented by the works of Aristotle ... In Aristotle's fundamental attitude toward the universe, in his affirmation of the concrete and sensuous reality of the world, Thomas recognized something entirely his own, belonging to himself as a Christian ... To put it in a nutshell this element was the same as the Christian affirmation of Creation.'[60]

(e) Thomas on Drinking and Drunkenness

One of the reasons given by the thirteenth-century Dominican Thomas of Cantimpré to explain why the friars made such a great intellectual impact on the University of Paris is that *they* 'kept vigil and studied',

[58] St Thomas Aquinas, *Lectura super Matthaeum*, p. 110. The quotation is from Aristotle's *Politics*, 1, 2.

[59] Josef Pieper, *Introduction to Thomas Aquinas* (London 1962) p. 132.

[60] *ibid.*, pp. 48-9.

whereas the other non-religious professors indulged themselves in so much eating and drinking at night that they were unable, in the morning, to make any notable impression.[61] That report is, of course, impressive. But, as one can imagine, with respect to Dominican drinking and Dominican vigils, it is not the whole story. As early as 1241, there was a complaint from the Provincial Chapter of Provence about 'nocturnal dinners and long confabulations' still going on after Compline.[62] And, in the Roman Province, a special rule had to be introduced which declared that the brethren must say Compline again after their nightly wine-drinking sessions![63]

[61] Cantimpré, *De Apibus*, II, x 31. See S. Tugwell, *Early Dominicans*, p. 107, n.27. Here the brethren were following Dominic's example, who 'drank wine so austerely diluted ... it never blunted his fine, sensitive spirit'. See *Jordan of Saxony: On the Beginnings of the Friars Preachers*, no.108, p. 27. See also *Vitae Fratrum*, V, 5, xiv, pp. 283-4.

[62] See S. Tugwell, *The Way of the Preacher* (London 1981) p. 57.

[63] Rome Chapter, 1251. See S. Tugwell, *The Way of the Preacher*, p. 57. We are told that in a certain house in France, on one occasion, the best wine was served by the woman of the house to Jordan of Saxony and his companions, a fact which greatly irritated the woman's husband! See *De vino meritis eius meliorato*, in *Vitae Fratrum*, XXXV, 3, p. 128. In another early story about Jordan, a certain Archdeacon, who particularly despised the Dominicans, complained that as soon as the preachers sat down at table they started drinking wine. Jordan did not deny this fact. But he did point out later to the Archdeacon that he had observed him, on one occasion, imbibing huge quanties of wine when at table with the friars, and not only during the meal but even before the meal got started. This observation from Jordan was enough, apparently, to silence the Archdeacon. See *Compilacio singularis exemplorum*, Uppsala, Bibliothèque universitaire, C.523, f.69. I am indebted to my confrère, Paul-Bernard Hodel O.P., for drawing my attention to this particular story.

Humbert of Romans, in his commentary on the *Rule*, complains that, on occasion, some of the brethren talk through 'almost an entire meal' concerning the merits of different wines, saying: 'This one is like that and the other like that, and so on.'[64] Humbert is clearly not impressed. He reports, with more than a hint of sarcasm, an incident in which 'a certain servant of God, finding himself, on one occasion, at table with a group of spiritual men who were talking on and on about wines, exclaimed: "For God's sake, dearly beloved, let's not talk so much about wines, but instead let's drink in better things – without so many words" '![65]

St Thomas Aquinas, like Humbert, as well as discussing drinking and drunkenness 'in the mystical sense', has a lot to say about drinking in its more ordinary manifestations. In fact, one entire question in the *Summa* (II II, q.150) is devoted exclusively to the subject of drunkenness. Wine in itself, in Thomas' view, is something entirely acceptable. 'Sober drinking,' he says,

[64] '*Epistola beati Humberti*,' LXIII, in *De vita regulari* (Rome 1888) p. 198.

[65] *ibid.*, p. 198. The Dominican enthusiasm for good wine clearly survived the centuries. John Henry Newman, when on a visit to Italy, was informed that the Dominicans 'at Florence and elsewhere' had preserved their own traditions. Naturally, Newman took this to mean that the Dominicans were perhaps 'still Thomists'. But, after further enquiry, he learned that 'the said Dominicans of Florence were manufacturers of scented water, etc and had very choice wines in their cellars'! See Newman's letter to J.D. Dalgairns, 18 October 1946, in *The Letters and Diaries of John Henry Newman*, vol. XI, C.S. Dessain (ed.) (London 1961) p. 263.

quoting Ecclesiasticus, 'is health for the body and soul.'[66]
The Oxford Dominican, Herbert McCabe, in a short
Catechism composed very much in the spirit of St
Thomas, asks the question: 'How do we exercise
temperateness in the matter of eating and drinking?'
And his answer: 'We exercise temperateness in the matter
of eating and drinking by, characteristically, taking and
enjoying what is sufficient for our health and for the
entertainment of our friends.'[67] Thomas himself remarks
in the *Summa*: 'if a person knows that, by refusing to take
wine, an oppressive burden will be placed on nature (*ut
naturam multum gravaret*) that person is not without
fault.'[68] Wine, it has to be said, though it may well be
health-giving, should not be over-indulged in, much less
regarded as one's best friend or one's only solace. 'Wine,'
Thomas remarks dryly, 'does not love man the way man
loves wine' (*Non enim vinum amat hominem, sicut homo
amat vinum*)![69] And again, in another place, quoting
Jerome, he writes: '*Venus is cold when Ceres and Bacchus
are not there*, that is to say lust is cooled by abstinence in
meat and drink.'[70]

The wine of wisdom which St Thomas was able to drink
in, day after day, year after year, though it may well have

[66] II II, q.149, a.1.

[67] Herbert McCabe, *The Teaching of the Catholic Church: A New
Catechism of Christian Doctrine*, no.240 (London 1991) p. 43.

[68] ST, II II, q.150, a.1, ad.1.

[69] St Thomas Aquinas, *Sententia libri ethicorum*, VIII, 2, 1115 b, 27
(Rome 1969) p. 446

[70] ST, II II, q.147, a.1. See further comments on drunkenness in
ST, I II, q.88, a.5, ad.1.

'intoxicated' him, did not abstract him into any kind of elitist reverie. Thomas kept his feet firmly planted on the ground. The few comments he makes about those who develop serious problems with drink are notable for their compassion and common sense. In this respect, Thomas' attitude recalls the great kindness and generosity of his predecessor in the Order, Jordan of Saxony. Jordan, we are told in *the Vitae Fratnum*, 'tried to correct faults more by winning gentleness and trusting his subjects than by harsh discipline ... He was love and mildness itself to the tempted and the sick, often brightening them with his cheery presence'.[71] On one occasion, wanting to welcome back into the Order a Dominican preacher who had gone seriously astray, Jordan consulted some of the friars. All agreed with the plan except one who refused to give his consent. Jordan argued his case, but to no avail.

> Still the brother would not yield, upon which the Master said impressively 'Ah brother, if you had shed but one drop of your blood for this poor man, as Christ has given the whole of his, you would look on the affair very differently.' At this truly touching appeal the other fell on his knees to beg forgiveness, and readily gave his consent.[72]

So consumed by love of neighbour was Jordan of Saxony that: 'often as he walked along the roads he would strip himself of his tunic to clothe some shivering beggar, for which the brethren used often chide him.'[73]

[71] *Vitae Fratrum*, III, 5, p. 103; P. Conway, *Lives*, p. 95.
[72] *ibid.*, III, 42, xxii, pp. 145-6; P. Conway, *Lives*, p. 128.
[73] *ibid.*, III, 4, p. 103; P. Conway, *Lives*, pp. 94-5.

An account has survived of a meeting one day between Jordan and a man very interested in alcohol. Hoping to get some money for drink, the man feigned sickness and poverty, so Jordan at once gave him one of his tunics. The man then went straight to the pub, and exchanged the tunic for a drink. 'The brethren, seeing this done, taunted Jordan with his naiveté: "There now, Master, see how wisely you have bestowed your tunic." "I did so," he said, "because I believed him to be in want through sickness and poverty, and it seemed at the moment to be a charity to help him; still, I reckon it better to have parted with my tunic than with my charity." '[74]

When, in the *Summa*, Aquinas refers to those individuals who have a problem with drink, the note of charity is again unmistakable. 'Such things as these,' he writes, 'are cured not by bitterness, severity, or harshness, but by teaching rather than commanding, by advice rather than threats.' And, he continues, 'such a course is to be followed with the majority of sinners: few are they whose sins should be treated with severity.'[75]

---

[74] *ibid.*, III, 42, vii, p. 140; P. Conway, *Lives*, p. 124. Jordan's concern for kindness to neighbour and the force of his wit are both evident in a comment he made once when he was preaching in England. His audience or congregation included a number of dignitaries, and they may have struck Jordan as being somewhat conceited. For, towards the end of his sermon, Jordan delivered a sharp rebuke to those 'who are so intent on the names of their ancestors they forget the names of their neighbours'! See Sermon 11: *In festo sancti Ioannis, die 27 decembris*, in Hoder, *Sermones*, p. 117.

[75] ST, II II, q.150, a.1, ad 4. St Thomas is quoting here from St Augustine's letter to Bishop Aurelius.

3. St Catherine of Siena: 'Drunk with Love'

Holy drunkenness is a theme which recurs over and over again in Catherine of Siena's letters. But when Catherine speaks of spiritual 'inebriation' and wholeheartedly recommends it, what she is hoping to see in others is not a wine of temporary elation, a mere drunkenness of feeling, but hearts and minds illumined and refreshed by the new wine of truth. Obedience to that truth and the surrender of one's life to the Word of life are what matter for Catherine.

(a) Letter to a Preacher

But, that being said, it is also important to note that, in Catherine's experience, the grace of faith-conviction is often accompanied by, and assisted by, the grace of an intense religious devotion or enthusiasm. This enthusiasm, though at times it can get out of hand, can be of enormous benefit to the preacher. In one of her letters, written to her close friend, the Dominican preacher Bartolomeo Dominici, Catherine speaks of 'a wine which intoxicates the soul so that the more one drinks of it the more one wants to drink'.[76] This 'wine' to which Catherine refers is a knowledge of God's love, a knowledge which she desires the preacher to drink in, at the table of the Lamb. 'Before I die,' she writes to Bartolomeo, 'I have desired with desire to celebrate [literally 'to do']

[76] Letter 208, in *Lettere di santa Caterina da Siena*, vol. III, N. Tommasèo (ed.) (Florence 1940) p. 212.

157

Easter with you.' And then she adds: 'This is the Easter I wish we could celebrate – to see one another at the table of the Immaculate Lamb.'[77] And again: 'the wine we discover at this table is the opened side of the Son of God.'[78]

Catherine is, of course, recalling here Chapter 18, verse 34 of St John's Gospel: 'They pierced his side, and immediately there flowed out blood and water.' One is inclined, at first, to recoil in horror from this image of utter and complete humiliation. But it was this event, more than any other, which became fundamental for Catherine's faith and hope. As she explained to Bartolomeo, here: 'the secret of the heart [of Christ] is laid bare.'[79] And, as she noted elsewhere in her writings, here the sins of the entire world are washed clean by the blood of the Lamb. Overwhelmed by this thought, Catherine turns in one of her prayers to Christ, and exclaims: 'stretched out on the cross you have embraced us. For you have made a cavern in your open side, where we might have a refuge.'[80] In her own deep humility, Catherine is the first to feel the need for this kind of grace or blessing. And so, having herself drunk deep from the wine of God's mercy, and found in Christ her true refuge, Catherine cannot rest until others have been helped to experience the same deep security in God's love, the same profound intoxication.

[77] ibid., p. 212.

[78] ibid., p. 213.

[79] ibid., p. 212.

[80] Prayer 19, in The Prayers of Catherine of Siena, trans., S. Noffke O.P. (New York 1983) p. 176.

(b) In Parenthesis: Eckhart and Tauler

Something of Catherine's passionate vision finds expression in the work of two other medieval Dominican mystics, Meister Eckhart and Johannes Tauler. Like Catherine, Eckhart believes that our love for God should be a kind of obsession or an addiction. Catherine had written to the preacher, Bartolomeo: 'Behave like someone who drinks a lot, and who becomes drunk and loses himself, and can't see himself any more.'[81] And, almost as if to match Catherine's appeal, Eckhart declares: 'A man ought not to love a God who is just a product of his thought ... because if the thought vanished, God too would vanish.'[82] God should be present to a man, Eckhart believes, so as to possess him and be possessed by him completely. 'It is,' he says, 'like a man consumed with a real and burning thirst, who may well not drink and may turn his mind to other things. But whatever he may do, in whatever company he may be, whatever he may be intending or thinking of or working at, still the idea of drinking does not leave him, so long as he is thirsty. The more his thirst grows, the more the idea of drinking grows and intrudes and possesses him and will not leave him.'[83]

Johannes Tauler, Meister Eckhart's most famous disciple, takes up the theme of spiritual drunkenness in one of his homilies. Throughout eternity, he states, 'we shall drink ... in long drafts from the fountainhead which

---

[81] Letter 208, in Tommasèo, *Lettre*, p. 212.

[82] *Counsels on Discernment*, no.6, in *Meister Eckhart: The Essential Sermons*, trans., E. Colledge and B. McGinn (London 1981) p. 253.

[83] *ibid.*, p. 253.

is God's paternal heart.' But, now, already in this life, 'we draw in as much as we can of this divine draft, and we become so filled with God that we forget ourselves in this overflowing bliss'.[84] In fact, so profound is this state, Tauler says, that sometimes 'a man will cry aloud, or sing or laugh'.[85] Sadly, however, Tauler notes, this kind of holy foolishness will inevitably provoke those 'reasonable people' who are 'ignorant of the wondrous ways of the Holy Spirit'. And they begin to make a fuss: '"Merciful heavens," they exclaim, "why are you carrying on in this ridiculous manner?" They do not see God's hand in it.' But of those people who are 'inebriated', Tauler says, 'love is aflame in them, and it glimmers and glows and consumes them with bliss'.[86] A remarkable ecstasy of this kind was experienced once in a dream-vision by the Dominican mystic and contemplative nun, Margaret Ebner, at the monastery of Maria Medingen in modern Bavaria. According to her own account she was allowed, for a few brief moments, to experience something of 'the joy and love' experienced by the saints in paradise. She writes:

> The choir was brightly illumined ... I saw many people behind the choir stalls dressed in white ... they all came running over to me with great joy. I was happy and thought I would say, 'Jesus Christ,' to see how they would respond ... they fell down on their knees with great desire and

[84] Sermon 11, in *Johannes Tauler: Sermons*, trans., M. Shrady (New York 1985) p. 57.
[85] *ibid.*, p. 58.
[86] *ibid.*, p. 58.

repeated, 'Jesus Christ,' and they sang with me. From that I gained such great grace and joy that I began to sing the sweet Name of Jesus Christ and they sang with me. And I said: 'We should dance.' Then they answered: 'We should dance and eat and drink with one another.'[87]

Johannes Tauler did not hesitate, in his writing, to offer a truly spirited defense of this kind of religious enthusiasm. But he is at pains also to sound a note of caution. He is aware that there are people who can sometimes get so carried away they need to be brought back to earth. They are like children, he says, who have gone down to their father's cellar, stolen the wine and got drunk. The father, as soon as he catches them, makes them suffer for their joys. And 'he gives them,' Tauler says, 'water to drink to make them as sober now as they were drunk before'.[88] Clearly, unlike St Catherine, Tauler does not have much very much practical knowledge of the state of drunkenness! But, in any case, he goes on at once to spell out what he means. The Lord, he says, 'withdraws … their strong wine,' that is he takes away 'their emotional comforts'. God 'allows them to grow as sad as they were joyful, as sober as they were drunk before'. And since, in their enthusiasm, they had lost all restraint, God 'wishes to recall them to sobriety. They are now sober … they have learned what their capabilities and limitations really are, and this makes them calm, sober and at peace'.[89]

[87] See *Margaret Ebner: Major Works*, Leonard P. Hindsley (ed.) (New York 1993) p. 163.

[88] Sermon 11, in *Johannes Tauler: Sermons*, p. 58.

[89] *ibid.*, p. 58-9.

161

In the view, then, of St Catherine of Siena and Blessed Johannes Tauler, both sobriety and drunkenness are needed: sobriety, so that we may stay close always to the knowledge of our own limitations, and drunkenness, so that we may 'get rid of all coldness',[90] and allow ourselves to become completely addicted to the Word of God and to the task of preaching the Word. According to Catherine the wine – Christ's blood – when it is drunk at the Eucharistic table gives not only 'joy to the heart and soul' of those who are present: it also 'restores the [preacher's] voice'.[91]

(c) The Drunkenness of God

One well-known effect of drinking is a marked increase in courage. 'Dutch courage,' it is called in Europe, and in North America they speak of the strength acquired from drink as 'beer muscles'. Catherine of Siena is well aware that no small courage was needed on occasion to preach the truth. And so, for this reason, she is instinctively drawn to the image or the metaphor of drinking, and she uses it to very considerable effect. Writing of Mary Magdalene, for example, Catherine says: 'She didn't think or worry about anything but how she could follow Christ ... She was no more self-conscious than a drunken woman.' Her only concern was 'how she might find and follow her Master.'[92]

---

[90] Letter 208, in Tommaseò, *Lettre*, p. 213.

[91] *ibid.*, p. 213.

[92] Letter to Monna Bartolemea di Selvatico of Lucca, in S. Noffke O.P. (trans.), *The Letters of St Catherine of Siena*, vol. 2 (Tempe, Arizona 2001) p. 42.

And again: 'She wasn't afraid of the Jews, nor did she fear for herself. No, like a passionate lover she ran and embraced the cross … *Surely you were drunk with love, O Magdalene!* As a sign that she *was* drunk with love for her Master, she showed it in her actions toward his creatures, when after his holy resurrection she preached [Christ risen].'[93]

The phrase 'drunk with love', repeated twice here, occurs elsewhere in Catherine's writings, but always in a rather astonishing context. For the one described as 'drunk with love' is not Mary Magdalene, or Catherine, or any other preacher of the Word, but … God himself! It is God, Catherine says, who is '*drunk with love* for our good'.[94] Stunned by this thought, she turns to God in one of her prayers, and exclaims:

> You, high eternal Trinity, acted as if you were drunk with love, infatuated with your creature … You, sweetness itself, stooped to join yourself with our bitterness. You, splendour, joined yourself with darkness; you, wisdom, with foolishness; you, life with death; you, the infinite, with us who are finite. What drove you to this?[95]

Catherine's amazed attention is focused here on the mystery of the Incarnation. But when she begins to meditate also on the mystery of the Cross, her language

[93] Letter to Monna Agnesa Malavolti and the *Mantellate* of Siena, in Noffke, *Letters*, p. 4. Following medieval tradition, Catherine regarded as the one person Mary Magdalene, Mary of Bethany, and the sinful woman who anointed the feet of Jesus.

[94] *The Dialogue*, 17, p. 55.

[95] Prayer 17, in Noffke, *Prayers*, p. 148.

becomes even more vivid: 'O priceless Love! You showed your inflamed desire when you ran like a blind and drunk man to the opprobrium of the cross. A blind man can't see, and neither can a drunk man when he is fast drunk. And thus he [Christ], almost like someone dead, blind and drunk, lost himself for our salvation'![96] In St Matthew's Gospel (Mt. 11:19) Christ is, of course, accused of being a 'drunkard'. And here, in this passage, what Catherine in effect is saying, is: Yes, his accusers were correct, in *one* sense at least, Jesus was indeed 'blind drunk' – but drunk with love for our salvation. 'O mad lover!' she cries out in *The Dialogue*, '... Why then are you so mad?' And the answer: 'Because you have fallen in love with what you have made! You are pleased and delighted over her within yourself, as if you were drunk for her salvation. She runs away from you and you go looking for her. She strays and you draw closer to her. You clothed yourself in our humanity, and nearer than that you could not have come.'[97]

Again and again Catherine's meditations on the mystery of the Incarnation and the Passion draw her thoughts back to the mystery of Creation. Why, if God foresaw how deep our failure would be, did he create us in the beginning? 'O unutterable love,' she exclaims, 'even

---

[96] Letter 225, in Tommasèo, *Lettere*, vol. III, p. 291.

[97] *The Dialogue*, 153, p. 325. One possible, non-Dominican source behind Catherine's teaching is Augustine's idea of Christ's passion as a form of drunken 'foolishness' (*ebrietas stultitiae*) in *Contra Faustum*, XII 24. Giacomo D'Urso suggests a Franciscan influence on St Catherine but seems unaware of the earlier Dominican use of the image of drinking. See *L'Ebrezza spirituale*, pp. 106-7.

though you saw all the evils that all your creatures would commit against your infinite goodness, you acted as if you did not see and set your eye only on the beauty of your creature, with whom you fell in love, like one drunk and crazy with love. And in love you drew us out of yourself giving us being.'[98] The mere thought of these things was enough, at times, to make Catherine feel dizzy or 'inebriated'. On the very last line of her *Dialogue* she confesses with astonishment and joy: 'I sense my soul once again becoming drunk! Thanks be to God!'[99]

Conclusion

A great variety of images has been used, over the centuries, to evoke aspects of the spiritual life: the ladder of perfection, for example; the dark night, the steep ascent of a mountain. But the Dominicans of the thirteenth and fourteenth centuries liked also, and with a distinct enthusiasm, it would appear, to make use of the image of drinking. They were drawn to it, I suspect, because it responded so well to their sense of the Gospel. Their spirituality was not something tense or introverted or self-preoccupied, but rather joyous and expansive. And so the image of a group of friends or companions drinking together would naturally have appealed to them. Wine or drink is an image of the goodness and sweetness of life. When St Dominic was alive, many of the ascetics of his time – and I am thinking here particularly of the

[98] Prayer 13, in Noffke, *Prayers*, pp. 112-13.
[99] *ibid.*, 167, p. 366.

Albigensians – regarded it, as they regarded food and sex, as something evil. But St Dominic, with his own deep understanding of the goodness of all creation, clearly accepted it as something wholesome and good.

Dominican preaching is sometimes described, and for good reason, as *doctrinal* since it delights in pondering and proclaiming the mysteries of Creation, Incarnation, Redemption and Resurrection. But the manner in which Dominican preachers, like Catherine and Thomas, speak about imbibing the wine of the mystery of Christ, alerts us to the fact that real 'knowing' is always accompanied by a certain amazement. The wine of truth which Christ gives us to drink is also a wine of astonishment. What we preach, then, are not just truths *about* God. We preach a wine of truth which we have actually tasted ourselves, and have drunk with living faith and joy.

The medieval Dominicans, being not only celebrants of grace but also defenders of nature, clearly loved the image of drinking and drunkenness because it gave them a vivid way of speaking about preaching – about the need, first, to become 'drunk' on the Word, and then about the effects of that encounter with God: the ecstasy of self-forgetfulness, the grace of new joy, the compulsion to share that joy with others, and the gifts of renewed hope and courage.

Of course, Dominicans were not the first people to speak about holy drinking. Centuries prior to the foundation of the Order, the image had already been used, and many times, by other Christian authors and preachers. Here, for example, is a short, beautiful passage from an anonymous homily inspired by Hippolytus. It concerns the mystery of the transformation of wine into the blood of Christ. The author notes: 'We are fed with the bread from heaven, our thirst is quenched with the cup of joy, the chalice afire with the Spirit, the blood wholly warmed from on high with the Spirit.'[100]

Dominicans, like everyone else in the Christian tradition, would have felt themselves instinctively drawn to the image of wine since it is an image which comes straight from the heart of the Gospel, and has a profound and direct link to the Eucharist. So it might seem, therefore, that one is mistaken to read too much into its use by Dominicans, especially since drinking wine was such a common practice in the Middle Ages. One might almost expect to find the image repeated everywhere in the mystical and spiritual literature of the period. But, curiously, in the *Fioretti* of St Francis of Assisi, for example, there is only one brief passage which refers to drinking. By contrast, in the early Dominican text, *Vitae Fratrum*, the image occurs again and again.[101]

Very often when people are thinking or speaking about the spirituality of the Dominican Order there is a

[100] 'Treatise on Easter', *Exordium* 8 (*Sources chrétiennes* 27, pp. 133 and 135) cited in Olivier Clément, *The Roots of Christian Mysticism: Texts from the Patristic Era with Commentary* (New York 1993) p. 113.

[101] As a help to understand Dominican spirituality, great and deserved attention has been given over the years to texts such as the *Summa* of Aquinas. But humble works such as the *Vitae* have also, I have discovered, their own usefulness and enchantment. To borrow a phrase from the author Robert Walser, works such as these are like 'old bottles of wine, which, to be sure, are drawn, only on particularly suitable occasions, out from under the dust, and so exalted to a place of honour'. See Walser, *Selected Stories* (Manchester 1982) p. 117.

tendency, with respect to a phrase such as 'sober intoxication', for example, to give more weight to the adjective 'sober' than to the noun 'intoxication'. It is an understandable tendency and, in respect of the work of many Dominican authors, often a wise one. The adjective 'sober' sits particularly well with the work of someone like St Thomas Aquinas, or with that of his contemporary, Humbert of Romans, or with the work of the later scholastics. But if one is considering the life and work of other Dominicans, such as the exuberant and generous preacher, Blessed Jordan of Saxony, or the irrepressible Italian mystic, St Catherine of Siena, or the colourful and intensely devout German friar, Blessed Henry Suso, or the great and daring thinker and visionary, Meister Eckhart, then clearly the word 'sober', for all its sane, and sharply qualifying wisdom, will need to have placed close beside it the noun 'intoxication'.

The Christian gospel has many humble and practical applications but, at its core, it contains a vision extravagant in range and scope. Well worth remembering, therefore, and especially in an age of *new* evangelization, are these words from Eric Hoffer's book, *The True Believer*. Hoffer writes: 'Those who would transform a nation or the world cannot do so by breeding and captaining discontent or by demonstrating the reasonableness and desirability of the intended changes or by coercing people into a new way of life. They must know how to kindle and fan an extravagant hope.'[102] It was no

---

[102] Eric Hoffer, *The True Believer: Thoughts on the Nature of Mass Movements* (New York 1951) p. 9.

accident that Pope Paul VI, when he was reflecting on the mystery of Christian hope, chose to define it as: 'hope for something that is not seen, and that *one would not dare imagine.*'[103] The Christian gospel is a gospel of vision or it is nothing at all.

There were many different kinds of men and women who followed faithfully the path of Dominic in the early centuries of the Order. But they did have one thing in common. All of them, after the example of Dominic, had learned to drink deep from the wine of God's Word. And they became, we can say, not only witnesses of certain great moral and doctrinal truths, but witnesses also of an unimaginable joy. To those who heard the Friars Preachers speak, for example, or who met them on their journeys, or who read their writings, it must have seemed, at times, as if simple, ordinary words had somehow caught fire – as after Pentecost – and were burning with a wisdom not of this earth. But what, we might ask, of the ministers of the Word today? Are there any who have the same capacity for vision, the same courage to proclaim to the world something more than the bland commonplaces

---

[103] Pope Paul VI, *Evangelii nuntiandi*, no.21. Italics added. Human beings, it is clear, cannot live without a vision of some kind or other, a fact underlined in an unusual statement about drunkenness by the Russian author Andrey Sinyavsky. Thinking about Russia in particular, Sinyavsky writes: 'Drunkenness is our basic national vice – more than this, our obsession. A simple Russian doesn't drink from wretchedness or to drown his cares, but because of his everlasting need for the miraculous, the extraordinary – he drinks mystically, if you like, in order to upset the earthly balance of his soul and restore it to its blissfully incorporeal state.' See Sinyavsky, *Unguarded Thoughts* (London 1974) p. 37.

of popular wisdom? Are we too sane and sensible to become drunk on the Word?

When in the *Summa* St Thomas is discussing the question of drunkenness, he all of a sudden surprises us by drawing attention to a vice or failure the very opposite of drunken excess, a vice which he says has no name, but which, perhaps, we might call *the vice of being too sober*.[104] Now being *too sober*, in relation to actually drinking alcohol, may or may not be a problem for preachers or pastors today! But, at the spiritual level, at the level of prayer-life and preaching, those who are ministers of the Word stand perhaps accused of being too sensible, too sober, too safe. Towards the end of his remarkable study, *Enthusiasm*, Ronald Knox writes: 'Men [and women] will not live without vision; that moral we do well to carry away with us from contemplating, in so many strange forms, the record of the visionaries. If we are content with the humdrum, the second-best, the hand-over-hand, it will not be forgiven us.'[105]

'Let us behave like the drunkard,' Catherine of Siena advises us. And she is not alone. Along with her, in many different forms, but always with something of the same impressive insistence, there speaks the witness – the teaching – of two centuries of Dominican tradition. 'Let us behave like the drunkard who doesn't think of himself but only of the wine he has drunk and of the wine that remains to be drunk'![106]

[104] ST, II II, q.150, a.1, ad.1.
[105] R. Knox, *Enthusiasm* (Oxford 1950) p. 591.
[106] Letter 29, Tommasèo, *Lettere*, vol. I, p. 108.

Bibliography

Abbreviations

AFP   *Archivum Fratrum Praedicatorum*
ASOP   *Analecta (Sacri) Ordinis Praedicatorum*
MOPH   *Monumenta Ordinis Praedicatorum Historica*
PL   Migne, *Patrologia Latina*
ST   St Thomas Aquinas, *Summae Theologiae*

Albert the Great, St, All works cited are from the *Opera Omnia* edition (1890-99) produced by Auguste Borgnet: *In Evangelicum secundum Matthaeum,* vol. XX; *Orationes super evangelia dominicalia,* vol. XIII; *De mineralibus,* vol. V; *Politica,* vol. VIII; *De caelo et mundo,* vol. IV; *De animalibus,* vol. XI.

Ashley, Benedict O.P., *The Dominicans,* (Collegeville MN 1990).

Aspiroz Costa, Carlos Alfonso, O.P., 'Libertad y responsabilidad dominicanas: Hacia una espiritualidad del gobierno', *Angelicum,* 81, 2 (2004), pp. 431-44.

Auden, W.H., *Another Time* (London 1940).

171

——*The Poet and the City*, in *Twentieth Century Poetry: Critical Essays and Documents*, G. Martin and P.N. Furbank (eds) (London 1975).

Augustine, St, *De moribus eccclesiae catholicae*, PL, 32.

Barron, Robert, *Thomas Aquinas: Spiritual Master* (New York 1996).

Barthélemy, Dominique O.P., 'The Responsibility of the Theologian', *Dominican Ashram*, X, 2 (1991) 67-9.

Bedouelle, Guy, O.P., *Saint Dominic: The Grace of the Word* (San Francisco 1987).

——'The Dominican Identity', *Dominican Ashram*, IX, 3 (1990) 130-40.

——'The Dominican Nuns: Historical Highlights, The Beginnings', *Dominican Ashram*, XI, 3 (1992) 108-18.

——*In the Image of St Dominic: Nine Portraits of Dominican Life* (San Francisco 1994).

——'Study in the Life of the Early Dominicans', *Dominican Ashram*, XIV, 4 (1995) 177-88.

Bedouelle, G., O.P. and Quilici A., O.P. (eds), *Les frères prêcheurs autrement dits Dominicains* (Paris 1997).

Bernal Palacios, Arturo O.P. (ed.) *Praedicatores inquisatores - I, The Dominicans and the Medieval Inquisition; Acts of the 1st International Seminar on the Dominicans and the Inquisition, 23-25 February 2002, Dissertationes Historicae*, XXIX (Rome 2004).

Borges, Jorge Luis, *The Argentine Writer and Tradition*, in *Labyrinths*, D.A. Yates (ed.) (New York 1962).

Bourke, V.J., *The Nicomachean Ethics and Thomas Aquinas*, in A.A. Maurer, (ed.) *St Thomas Aquinas: Commemorative Studies* (Toronto 1974).

Boyle, Leonard E., O.P., *The Dominican Order and Theological Study* (New York 1995).

—*Aux origins de la liturgie Dominicaine,* edited with P-M. Guy, O.P. (Paris 2004).

Burke, Thomas, N., O.P., *Lectures and Sermons* (New York 1905).

Byrne, Damian, O.P., 'On the Role of Study in the Order', in *To Praise, To Bless, To Preach: Words of Grace and Truth* (Dublin 2004) pp. 267–76.

Camacho, Pedro José Diaz O.P. (ed.) *Pasión por la verdad: el studio en el carisma dominicano* (Bucaramanga 2000).

Catherine of Siena, St., *Le Lettere di S. Caterina da Siena,* (6 vols), N. Tommasèo (ed.) (Florence 1940).

—*Il Dialogo della divina providenza,* G. Cavallini (ed.) (Rome 1968).

—*Le Orazioni,* G. Cavallini (ed.) (Rome 1978).

—*The Dialogue,* trans., S. Noffke O.P. (New York 1980).

—*The Prayers of Catherine of Siena,* trans., S. Noffke O.P. (New York 1983).

—*The Letters of St Catherine of Siena,* trans., S. Noffke. Two of four projected volumes of the complete letters translated into English have already appeared (Tempe, Arizona 2000 and 2001).

Cavallini, Giuliana, *St Martín de Porres: Apostle of Charity* (New York 1979).

Cecilia, Blessed, 'The Legend of St Dominic by Blessed Cecilia', in *The Lives of the Brethren,* trans., P. Conway (London 1955) pp. 69–89. The original text edited by A. Walz, *Miracula b. Dominici,* AFP, XXXVII (1967), 5ff.

Chenu, M-D. O.P., 'The Revolutionary Intellectualism of St. Albert', *Blackfriars*, 19 (1938) 5-15.

Chesterton, G.K., *St Thomas Aquinas* (London 1933).

——*Collected Works* vol. I, D. Dooley (ed.) (San Francisco 1986).

Clément, Olivier, *The Roots of Christian Mysticism: Texts from the Patristic Era with Commentary* (New York 1993).

Congar, Yves O.P., *Lay People in the Church: A Study for a Theology of Laity*, (London 1959).

——'Action et contemplation: D'une lettre du père Congar au père Régamey (1959)', *La Vie spirituelle*, 152, 727 (1998) p. 204-5.

——*Les Voies du Dieu vivant: théologie et vie spirituelle* (Paris 1962).

——*Faith and Spiritual Life*, trans., A. Manson (London 1969).

——*'In dulcedine societatis quaerere veritatem': Notes sur le travail en équipe chez S. Albert et chez les prêcheurs au XIII siècle*, in Meyer, G. and Zimmermann, A. (eds) *Albertus Magnus Doctor Universalis* (Mainz, 1980), 47-57.

——*Called to Life* (New York 1985).

——*Sacramental Worship and Preaching* in *The Renewal of Preaching: Theory and Practice*, K. Rahner (ed.) (New York 1993), pp. 51-63.

——*Journal d'un théologien, 1946-1956* (Paris 2001).

D'Amato, Alfonso O.P., *Il Fascino della verità: Beato Giordano di Sassonia* (Bologna 1991).

——*Il Progetto di san Domenico* (Bologna 1994).

Dante Alighieri, *The Divine Comedy* (3 vols) (Oxford 1971).

Dostoyevsky, Fyodor, *The Brothers Karamazov* (New York 1972).

D'Urso, Giacinto O.P., *L'Ebrezza spirituale (o sobria ebrietas) in S. Caterina*, in T. Centi O.P. (ed.) *S. Caterina tra i dottori della chiesa* (Florence 1970), 103-14.

Duval, André O.P., *L'étude dans la legislation religieuse de s. Dominique*, in *Mélanges offerts à M.D. Chenu* (Paris 1967), 221-47.

Dwyer, Malachy O.P., 'Reclaiming the Dominican Vision for the 21st Century: Pursuing Communion in Government, Role of Community Chapter', *Dominican Ashram*, XV, 2 (1996) 78-89.

Ecclestone, A., *A Staircase for Silence* (London 1977).

Eckhart, Meister, *Meister Eckhart: A Modern Translation*, trans., R.B. Blakney (New York 1941).

——*Meister Eckhart: An Introduction to his Works with an Anthology of His Sermons*, trans., J.M. Clark (London 1957).

——*Meister Eckhart, Deutsche Mystiker des Mittelalters Meister Eckhart, Deutsche Mystiker des Mittelalters*, Bd. 2, F. Pfeiffer (ed.) (Leipzig 1857; repr. Scientia Verlag. Aalen 1962).

——*Meister Eckhart: Sermons and Treatises* (3 vols.), M. O'C. Walshe (ed.) (Longmead 1979, 1981, 1987).

——*Meister Eckhart: The Essential Sermons, Commentaries, Treatises and Defense,* trans., E. Colledge and B. McGinn (London 1981).

——*Maître Eckhart: Traites et sermons*, trans., A. de Libera (Paris 1993).

Eliot, T.S., *The Complete Poems and Plays of T.S. Eliot*, (London 1969).

BIBLIOGRAPHY

Emery, K. and Wawrykow, J.P. (eds) *Christ among the Medieval Dominicans* (Notre Dame, Indiana 1998).

Foster, Kenelm O.P. (ed.) *The Life of St Thomas Aquinas: Biographical Documents* (London 1959).

Fry, Timothy O.S.B. (ed.), *The Rule of St Benedict* (Collegeville 1981).

Fuente, Antolín González O.P., *El estudio asiduo de la verdad sagrada*, in *El carisma de la vida dominicana* (Salamanca 1994), 183-97.

Gerard de Frachet, *Vitae Fratrum*, B.M. Reichert, O.P. (ed.), MOPH, I (Louvain 1896).

——*The Lives of the Brethren*, trans., Placid Conway (London 1955).

Gui, Bernard, *Vita s. Thomae Aquinatis*, in *Fontes vitae*, fasc.III; documents edited from the *Revue thomiste*, 1913-1927; trans., Kenelm Foster, O.P. in *The Life of Saint Thomas Aquinas: Biographical Documents* (London 1959), 25-81.

Gutiérrez, Gustavo O.P., *Las Casas: In Search of the Poor of Christ* (New York 1993).

Hebblethwaite, Peter, *Pope John XXIII: Pope of the Council* (London 1984).

Hinnebusch, William A. O.P., *The History of the Dominican Order,* 2 vols (New York 1966, 1973).

Hoffer, Eric, *The True Believer: Thoughts on the Nature of Mass Movements* (New York 1951).

Hopkins, G.M., *The Poetical Works of Gerard Manley Hopkins* (Oxford 1990).

Humbert of Romans, *Opera de vita regulari*, 2 vols, J.J. Berthier (ed.) (Rome 1888, 1889).

——*Treatise on the Formation of Preachers*, in S. Tugwell, *Early Dominicans: Selected Writings* (New York 1982).

Jarrett, Bede O.P., *Meditations for Layfolk* (London 1946).

——*An Anthology of Bede Jarrett*, J. Aumann (ed.) (Dubuque 1961).

Jordan of Saxony, *Libellus de principiis ordinis praedicatorum*, M-H. Laurent O.P. (ed.), MOPH, XVI (Rome 1935).

——*Beati Iordani De Saxonia epistulae*, A. Walz O.P. (ed.), MOPH XXIII (Rome 1951).

——*Love Among the Saints: The Letters of the Blessed Jordan of Saxony to Blessed Diana of Andalò*, K. Pound (ed.) (London 1959).

——*To Heaven with Diana: A Study of Jordan of Saxony and Diana d'Andalò with a translation of the Letters of Jordan*, Gerald Vann O.P. (ed. and trans.) (London 1960).

——*Jordan of Saxony: On the Beginnings of the Order of Preachers*, trans., S. Tugwell (Dublin 1982).

——*Beati Iordani de Saxonia: Sermones*, Paul-Bernard Hodel O.P. (ed.), MOPH, XXIX (Rome 2005).

——'Encyclical Letter, May 1233', in S. Tugwell, *Early Dominicans: Selected Writings* (New York 1982), 122-5.

Just, Claude (A-M Roguet O.P.), *Saint Albert le Grand célébré par personnages* (Paris 1932).

Knox, Ronald, *Enthusiasm* (Oxford 1950).

Kochanievicz, Boguslaw O.P., 'The Contribution of the Dominicans to the Development of the Rosary', *Angelicum*, 81, 2 (2004) 377-403.

Koudelka, Vladimir O.P., *Dominic* (London 1997).

Lehner, F.C. O.P. (ed.), *Saint Dominic: Biographical Documents* (Washington 1964).

BIBLIOGRAPHY

Little, A.G., 'Three Sermons of Friar Jordan of Saxony, the Successor of St Dominic, preached in England, A.D. 1229', *The English Historical Review*, CCXIII (1939) 1-19.

Mandonnet, Pierre O.P., *St. Dominic and His Work*, (London 1944).

Margaret Ebner, *Margaret Ebner: Major Works*, L.P. Hindsley O.P. (ed.) (New York 1993).

McCabe, Herbert O.P., *The Teaching of the Catholic Church: A New Catechism of Christian Doctrine* (London 1991).

McNabb, Vincent O.P., *A Vincent McNabb Anthology: Selections from the Writings of Vincent McNabb O.P.*, F.E. Nugent (ed.) (London 1955).

—*The Craft of Prayer* (London 1935).

—*The Craft of Suffering* (London 1936).

—*An Old Apostle Speaks: Father Vincent McNabb O.P.*, Gerald Vann O.P. (ed.) (Oxford 1946).

Mechtild Of Magdeburg, *The Flowing Light of the Godhead*, trans., F. Tobin (New York 1998).

Merton, Thomas, *No Man is an Island* (New York 1955).

Meyer, G. and Zimmermann, A. (eds), *Albertus Magnus Doctor Universalis 1280/1980* (Mainz 1980).

Mills, John Orme O.P. (ed.) *Justice, Peace and the Dominicans 1216-2001* (Dublin 2002).

Monk, Ray, *Ludwig Wittgenstein: The Duty of Genius* (London 1991).

Morenzoni, Franco, 'Les Sermons de Jourdain de Saxe, successeur de saint Dominique', AFP, vol. LXVI, 1996, 201-44.

Mulchahey, M. Michèle, '*First the Bow is Bent in Study': Dominican Education before 1350* (Toronto 1998).

Murray, Paul O.P., '[Meister Eckhart]: The Way of the Void', in *New Blackfriars*, 74, 69 (1993) 116-30. First published in *Eckhart Review* (March 1993), 3-17.

Newman, John Henry, *The Mission of St Benedict*, in *Historical Sketches*, vol. 2 (Westminster, Maryland 1970; first published, 1858), 363-430.

——'Feasting in Captivity', Sermon XXV, in *Sermons Bearing on Subjects of the Day* (London 1869), 381-94.

——*The Letters and Diaries of John Henry Newman*, vol. XI, C.S. Dessain (ed.) (London 1961).

Nietzsche, Friedrich, *The Anti-Christ*, (Harmondsworth 1968).

Nolan, Albert O.P., 'Spiritual Growth and the Option for the Poor', *Dominican Ashram*, V, 3 (1986) 107-14.

Peraldus, William, *Sermon on Prayer*, in *Early Dominicans*, S. Tugwell (ed.), 163-77.

Pieper, Josef, *Introduction to Thomas Aquinas*, (London 1962).

——*Josef Pieper: An Anthology* (San Francisco 1984).

——*A Brief Reader on the Virtues of the Human Heart* (San Francisco 1991).

Pinckaers, Servais O.P., *The Sources of Christian Ethics* (Edinburgh 1995).

——*The Pursuit of Happiness* (New York 1998).

Principe, W.H., *Thomas Aquinas' Spirituality* (Toronto 1984).

Radcliffe, Timothy, O.P., 'An Integral Dominican Formation', *Dominican Ashram*, XIV, 1 (1995) 51-7.

——Letter to the Rector of the University of St Thomas,

Manila, 20 January 1997, ASOP, 105, fasc.I (January-April 1997), 33-4.

——*Sing a New Song: The Christian Vocation* (Dublin 1999).

Raymond of Capua, St, *The Life of Catherine of Siena*, trans., C. Kearns O.P. (Wilmington 1980).

Rilke, Rainer Maria, *Letters of Rainer Maria Rilke* (New York 1945).

Russell, Kenneth C., 'Get Serious! The Monastic Condemnation of Laughter', *Review for Religious* (May-June 1993) 371-9.

Sanderlin, G. (ed.), *Bartolomé de las Casas: A Selection of His Writings* (New York 1971).

Sertillanges, A.D. O.P., *The Intellectual Life* (Cork 1965).

Sheppard, L.C., *Lacordaire: A Biographical Essay* (New York 1904).

Sinyavsky, Andrey, *Unguarded Thoughts* (London 1974).

Solignac, Aimé, 'Ivresse spirituelle', in *Dictionnaire de spiritualité*, vol. VII (Paris 1971), 2312-37.

Suso, Henry, *The Life of the Servant*, trans., J.M. Clark (London 1952).

——*Henry Suso: The Exemplar with Two German Sermons*, F. Tobin (ed.) (New York 1989).

Tauler, Johannes, *Johannes Tauler: Sermons*, M. Shrady (ed.) (New York 1985).

Teresa of Avila, St., *Obras de Santa Teresa de Jesus*, Silverio de Santa Teresa O.C.D. (ed.) (Burgos 1915).

Thomas À Kempis, *The Imitation of Christ*, trans., R. Challoner (Dublin 1915).

Thomas Aquinas, St: unless otherwise indicated all references are to the *Summa Theologiae* edited with English translation (London and New York 1964-80).

Other works cited are: *Sententia super metaphysicam* (Marietti edition); *Contra impugnantes Dei cultum et religionem* (Leonine edition); *Sententia libri ethicorum* (Leonine edition); *Opuscula alia dubia* (Parma edition); *Opuscula vix dubia* (Mandonnet edition); *Summa contra Gentiles* (Leonine edition); *Expositio in librum b. Dionysii de divinis nominibus* (Marietti edition); *Super Boethium de Trinitate* (Leonine edition); *Postilla super Psalmos* (Parma edition); *Super Evangelium Johannis* (Marietti edition); *Expositio super Isaiam ad litteram* (Leonine edition); *Lectura super Matthaeum* (Parma edition); *Index thomisticus: S. Thomae Aquinatis Opera omnia,* vol.6 (Busa edition).

––*Commentary on the Gospel of John*, trans., J.A. Weisheipl, O.P. (New York 1980).

Thomas of Cantimpré, *Defense of the Mendicants*, in S. Tugwell, *Early Dominicans*, 133–6.

––*Bonum universale de apibus* (Douais 1627).

Tillard, J.M.R. O.P., *Théologie et vie ecclèsiale*, in *Initiation à la pratique de la théologie*, vol. I, B. Laurent and F. Refoulé (eds) (Paris 1982), 172–7.

Tillich, Paul, *The Boundaries of our Being* (London 1973).

Torrell, Jean-Pierre O.P., *Saint Thomas d'Aquin, vol.1, Initiation à saint Thomas d'Aquin* (Paris 1993); published in English as *St Thomas Aquinas: The Person and His Work* (Washington 1996).

––*Saint Thomas d'Aquin, vol. 2, Maître spirituel* (Fribourg 1996); published in English as *St Thomas Aquinas: Spiritual Master* (Washington 2003).

––'Ascèse intellectuelle et vie spirituelle', in *La Vie spirituelle*, 153, 733 (1999), 611–21.

Tugwell, Simon, O.P., *The Way of the Preacher* (London 1981).

——*Early Dominicans: Selected Writings* (New York 1982).

——'A Dominican Theology of Prayer', *Dominican Ashram,* I, 3 (1982) 128-44.

——*Scholarship, Sanctity and Spirituality* (Gonzaga University, Spokane 1983).

——'Dominic the Founder - I', *Dominican Ashram*, IV, 2 (1985) 80-96.

——'Dominic the Founder - II', *Dominican Ashram*, IV, 3 (1985) 122-45.

——'The Mendicants' and 'The Dominicans', in *The Study of Spirituality*, C. Jones, G. Wainwright and E. Yarnold (eds) (Oxford 1986), 294-95 and 296-300.

——*Albert and Thomas: Selected Writings* (New York 1988).

——'Friars and Canons: The Earliest Dominicans', in Judith Loades (ed.) *Monastic Studies*, II (Bangor 1991), 193-207.

——'Notes on the Life of St Dominic', AFP, LXV (1995) 5-169; LXVI (1996) 5-200; LXVII (1997) 27-59; LXVIII (1998) 5-116.

——'Dominican Spirituality', in *Compendium of Spirituality*, vol. II, E. De Cea, O.P. (ed.) (New York 1996), 117-47.

——'The Genesis of the Order of Preachers - I', *Dominican Ashram*, XVI, 2 (1997) 78-88.

——*St Dominic and the Order of Preachers* (Dublin 2001).

Vicaire, M-H. O.P., *Saint Dominic and His Times* (Green Bay, Wisconsin 1964); a translation of the first edition of *Histoire de Saint Dominique* (Paris 1982).

——'A Commentary on the Basic Constitution of the Friars Preachers', *Dominican Ashram*, 1, 1 (1982), 29-44.

—*The Genius of St Dominic* (Nagpur 1990).

Villot, Jean Cardinal, '*Homelia in Basilica Sanctae Sabinae*', ASOP, 39 (July-September 1970), 541–3.

Wallace, William, A., *The Scientific Methodology of St. Albert the Great*, in *Albertus Magnus Doctor Universalis 1280/1980*, G. Meyer and A. Zimmermann (eds) (Mainz 1980), 385–407.

Walser, Robert, *Selected Stories* (Manchester 1982).

Walsh, Liam G. O.P., *St. Thomas and Study*, in *La Formazione integrale domenicana*, R. Christian O.P. (ed.) (Bologna 1996), 228ff. An earlier version of this paper was published in *The Renewal Papers* (Tallaght 1994), 58–89.

Weil, Simone, *The Notebooks*, vol. 2 (New York 1956).

—*Waiting on God* (Glasgow 1983).

Weisheipl, James O.P., *The Place of Study in the Ideal of St. Dominic* (River Forest 1960).

—*Friar Thomas d'Aquino: His Life, Thought and Works* (Washington 1983).

—*Mystic on Campus: Friar Thomas*, in *An Introduction to the Medieval Mystics of Europe*, Paul Szarmach (ed.) (New York 1984), 135–59.

White, Patrick, 'The Prodigal Son', in *Australian Letters*, vol. 1, 3 (1958), 37–40.

BIBLIOGRAPHY

White, Victor O.P., 'The Letter of St. Thomas to Brother John: *De modo studendi*', in *Life of the Spirit: Blackfriars*, (1944 Suppl.) 161-80.

William of Tocco, *Vita s. Thomae Aquinatis*, D. Prümmer (ed.), fasc. II, in *Fontes vitae s. Thomae Aquinatis*; documents edited from the *Revue thomiste*, 1913-27.

Wilms, Hieronymus O.P., *Albert the Great: Saint and Doctor of the Church* (London 1933).

Woods, Richard O.P., *Mysticism and Prophecy: The Dominican Tradition* (London 1998).

Biographical Notes on Dominican Men and Women

ALBERT THE GREAT, ST (c.1199-1280)

Doctor of the Church and patron saint of scientists. Although an outstanding intellectual in his own right, he is perhaps best known as the teacher of St Thomas Aquinas. He combined a notable genius for natural science together with a proficiency in all branches of theology and philosophy. No man was more possessed with curiosity concerning the workings of the natural and supernatural worlds. See S. Tugwell, *Albert the Great*, in *Albert and Thomas: Selected Writings* (New York 1988) pp. 1-129.

BARTOLOMÉ DE LAS CASAS (1474-1566)

Spanish Dominican. Author and Missionary. A courageous preacher of justice, he was appalled at the treatment of the native population in the New World and sought to reform the early colonial practice. See *Bartolomé de las Casas: A Selection of His Writings*, G. Sanderlin (ed.) (New York 1971).

BARTOLOMEO DOMINICI (1343-1415)

A native of Siena, he was introduced to St Catherine of Siena when, by his own account, he was 24 years old and she was about 21. He accompanied Catherine on a number of her journeys, and served occasionally as her confessor. After Catherine's death he was active in the reform movement in Italy.

BURKE, THOMAS (1830-1883)

Irish Dominican. Greatly admired for the eloquence of his preaching and for his wit and good humour, he became a legendary communicator of the Catholic faith. In the end, having spent himself utterly, on both sides of the Atlantic, in the task of preaching, he died relatively young and is buried at Tallaght near Dublin in the Dominican Priory Church. See Thomas N. Burke, *Lectures and Sermons* (New York 1905).

CATHERINE OF SIENA, ST (1347-1380)

Mystic and Doctor of the Church, she exercised a very considerable influence on her contemporaries, and was partly responsible for the return of Pope Gregory XI from Avignon to Rome. Many of her letters have survived. Her most celebrated work, *Il Dialogo della divina Providenza*, is translated by Suzanne Noffke, O.P. (New York 1980). A complete translation of all the letters and prayers of Catherine has been undertaken in recent years by Noffke.

CECILIA, BL. (c.1202-1290)

She was the first of the reformed community of nuns at San Sisto established by St Dominic in 1221. Later she became prioress at Bologna. Stories which she told about

St Dominic, and which she may have dictated in her old age, are gathered together in a text known as *The Miracles of Blessed Dominic.*

CHENU, MARIE-DOMINIQUE (1895–1990)
Theologian and Medievalist. In his writing and teaching at *Le Saulchoir* near Paris he challenged the non-historical exposition of Thomism expressed by his teacher in Rome, P. Garrigou-Lagrange, and sought to replace it by reading St Thomas in his historical context.

CONGAR, YVES (1904–1995)
French Theologian and Ecumenist. The list of Congar's published titles exceeds 1,700 books and articles. As a theologian at the Second Vatican Council he made a major contribution. In 1994 Pope John Paul II appointed him to the College of Cardinals.

DIANA D'ANDOLÒ, BL.
A contemplative Dominican nun, she made a vow of religion to St Dominic in 1219. With four companions, she established a convent at Bologna in 1223. Approximately 50 letters sent to her, and to her community, from her beloved friend, Jordan of Saxony, have survived (see under JORDAN OF SAXONY).

DOMINIC, ST (1170–1221)
Founder of the Order of Preachers. Born in Caleruega, Old Castille, Spain. In addition to the friars he helped establish an Order of enclosed Dominican nuns. An 'evangelical man', single-minded in his determination to be a preacher of the Gospel, Dominic was remarkable for his dedication to prayer, his fearlessness and radiant joy,

his zeal for souls and his quick and generous response to the needs of the hour. He was canonized in 1234. See Vladimir Kouldelka O.P., *Dominic* (London 1997); Guy Bedouelle O.P., *St Dominic: The Grace of the Word* (San Francisco 1987); Simon Tugwell O.P., *St Dominic and the Order of Preachers* (Dublin 2001).

ECKHART, MEISTER (c.1260-1327)

One of the most remarkable preachers and mystics of the Middle Ages. His devotion to a radical form of the *via negativa* and his love of paradox and speculation resulted in the condemnation (within one diocese) of certain of his teachings. He himself was never excommunicated, nor did the Church ever forbid the reading of his works. What is more, although the condemnation has never been officially abrogated, his own personal fidelity to orthodox belief is today acknowledged by most scholars. Pope John Paul II, at an audience in September 1985, drew attention to the spiritual depth and humanity of Eckhart's mysticism: 'Did not Eckhart teach his disciples: "All that God asks you most pressingly is to go out of yourself ... and let God be God in you." One could think that in separating himself from creatures, the mystic leaves his brothers, humanity, behind. The same Eckhart affirms that, on the contrary, the mystic is marvellously present to them on the only level where he can truly reach them, that is, in God.' See *L'Osservatore Romano,* 28 October, 1985.

GERALD DE FRACHET (1205-1271)

A fine preacher, he entered the Order in Paris in 1225, making his profession to Jordan of Saxony. Best known for being the compiler of the *Vitae Fratrum* (*The Lives of the Brethren*).

GUI, BERNARD (c.1261–1331)
A French Dominican and an important historian of the Order. He ended his days as a bishop.

HENRY OF COLOGNE
Entered the Order in Paris in 1220. A great preacher. His friend, Jordan of Saxony, wrote of him: 'He was so affable that, if you spent even a little time with him, you would come away thinking that you were the friend he loved most in the world.'

HUGH OF ST CHER (†1264)
A Doctor of Canon Law and a Bachelor of Theology at Paris, he entered the Order there in 1225. He was made a Cardinal in 1244. With the help of fellow Dominicans in Paris he compiled an enormous commentary on the Bible.

HUMBERT OF ROMANS, BL. (c.1200–1277)
Born at Romans in France, he became Master of the Order in 1254. An efficient organiser and a man of great common sense, he helped to give shape to many different aspects of the Order's life. He wrote a commentary on *The Rule of St Augustine* and a *Letter on Regular Observance*. A much overlooked but important work is his *Treatise on the Formation of Preachers*.

HUTCHINSON, CATHAL (1918–2000)
Irish Dominican. A preacher gifted with a great sense of humour and a lively theological intelligence. Although a lover of all forms of literature, he wrote no books himself.

His own 'writing' – the testament he left behind – like that of the majority of preachers in every age, including Dominic himself, is what survives in the minds and hearts of those who heard his preaching or who were fortunate enough to have known him.

JARRETT, BEDE (1881–1934)
Provincial of the English Province from 1916 to 1932, he was a born leader. Under his inspiration the Dominicans returned to Edinburgh and Oxford. Among other works he published a life of St Dominic. See *An Anthology of Bede Jarrett*, J. Aumann O.P. (ed.) (Dubuque 1961).

JORDAN OF SAXONY, BL. (†1237)
Second Master of the Dominican Order. A preacher of joy and a man of enormous courage and compassion, he is by far the most attractive figure among the early Dominicans. His letters to his close friend, the contemplative nun, Diana d'Andolò, are distinguished by their great practical wisdom and human warmth. See G. Vann, O.P., *To Heaven with Diana: A Study of Jordan of Saxony and Diana d'Andalò with a translation of the Letters of Jordan* (New York 1960).

LACORDAIRE, HENRI DOMINIQUE (1802–1861)
One of the most famous preachers of the nineteenth century, he helped re-establish the French Dominican Province. See L.C. Sheppard, *Lacordaire: A Biographical Essay* (New York 1964).

LAGRANGE, MARIE-JOSEPH (1855–1938)
A brilliant Scripture scholar and saintly Dominican, he spent many years at the École Biblique in Jerusalem. In

the early years of the twentieth century he lifted, almost single-handedly, Catholic Biblical studies out of mediocrity. His cause for beatification has been introduced.

MARGARET EBNER (1291-1351)
A Dominican nun and mystic at the Monastery of Maria Medingen near Dillengen on the Danube. Renowned for great holiness, she taught the centrality of a personal relationship with Christ. See *Margaret Ebner: Major Works*, L.P. Hindsley (ed.) (New York 1993).

MARTíN DE PORRES, ST (1579-1639)
A Dominican Lay-Brother, he was born at Lima, Peru, and joined the Order at the age of 15. Dedicated to those people who were regarded as the dregs of society, he provided food, clothing and medicine. A preacher in his own right, the kindness he showed to those in need was far more eloquent of God than any words. He was canonized on 6 May 1962. See Giuliana Cavallini, *St Martín de Porres: Apostle of Charity* (New York 1970).

MCNABB, VINCENT (1868-1943)
Born in Northern Ireland, and educated at St Malachy's College, Belfast, he joined the English Dominican Province in 1885. Although he wrote several books, he was known first and last as a preacher. A considerable number of his contemporaries regarded him as a saint. G.K. Chesterton wrote: 'He is one of the few great men I have met in my life … nobody who ever met or saw or heard Father McNabb has ever forgotten him.' See *A Vincent McNabb Anthology: Selections from the Writings of Vincent McNabb, O.P.*, F.E. Nugent (ed.) (London 1955).

MECHTILD OF MAGDEBURG (c.1212-c.1294)
The little information we have about Mecthtild comes largely from her own mystical work, *The Flowing Light of the Godhead*. Her younger brother was a Dominican, and she herself enjoyed for years a close contact with the Dominican Order. Her confessor (probably the Dominican Heinrich of Halle) encouraged her to keep a record of her many visions. When she was already advanced in years, she entered the Cistercian convent of Helfta. See *Mechtild of Magdeburg: The Flowing Light of the Godhead*, F. Tobin (ed.) (New York 1977).

PERALDUS, WILLIAM († after 1261)
An influential preacher and moralist, his *Summa on the Vices and Virtues* enjoyed enormous success in the Middle Ages.

RAYMOND OF CAPUA, BL. (c.1330-1399)
Originally destined for a legal career, he joined the Order instead, and became one of the most prominent Dominicans of his generation. He was appointed spiritual confessor to St Catherine of Siena, and shortly after her death in 1380 he was elected Master of the Order. His life of Catherine (*Legenda major*) has been translated by Conleth Kearns O.P. as *The Life of St Catherine of Siena by Raymond of Capua* (Wilmington 1980).

REGINALD OF ORLEANS, BL. (†1220)
Shortly after entering the Order, St Dominic put him in charge in Bologna. His inspired preaching inspired Jordan of Saxony to join the Dominicans. In his *Libellus* Jordan writes that Reginald 'threw himself utterly into

preaching', and with so much energy the people of Bologna thought 'a new Elijah' had arisen among them.

SERTILLANGES, ANTONIN-GILBERT (1863-1948)
French Dominican. Best known for his book *The Intellectual Life*. His writing is characterized by breadth of thought and by a generous Christian humanism.

SUSO, HENRY, BL. (c.1295-1366)
Mystic and Preacher. A disciple of Meister Eckhart. Part of his work as a Dominican involved preaching to a group called the Friends of God and to enclosed Dominican contemplatives. His theology is less speculative than that of Eckhart, and is marked by a tender, personal love for the humanity of Christ. See *Henry Suso: The Exemplar with Two German Sermons*, F. Tobin (ed.) (New York 1989).

TAULER, JOHANNES, BL. (c.1300-1361)
Preacher and Mystic. Although a disciple of the teaching of Eckhart, Tauler's sermons are noted more for their warmth and moderation than for their speculative daring. See *Johannes Tauler: Sermons,* M. Shadry (ed.) (New York 1985).

THOMAS AQUINAS, ST (c.1225-1274)
Honoured under the titles 'Angelic Doctor', 'Common Doctor', and, more recently, 'Doctor of Humanity', he is considered the greatest of the medieval theologians. Acknowledging always the primacy of revelation, he nevertheless recognized the autonomy proper to human reason, and emphasized the importance of philosophy in the study of theology. See Jean-Pierre Torrell, O.P., *St Thomas Aquinas, vol. 1: The Person and the Work*

(Washington 1996) and *St Thomas Aquinas, vol. 2: Spiritual Master* (Washington 2003). See also S. Tugwell, *Thomas Aquinas*, in *Albert and Thomas: Selected Writings* (New York 1988), 199–351.

THOMAS OF CANTIMPRÉ (c.1201–c.1276)
Hagiographer and Encyclopedist. Originally an Augustinian Canon, he became a Dominican c.1230. His engaging but somewhat credulous book *Bonum universale de apibus* (1256–1261) contains much interesting historical information.

WILLIAM OF TOCCO
He lived for two years (1272–1273) with St Thomas Aquinas at San Domenico in Naples, and later wrote one of the early biographies of Thomas.

Index

INDEX